Southern Get-Togethers

Southern Get-Togethers

A Guide to Hosting Unforgettable Gatherings

Plus Entertaining Inspiration,
Tips, and 100+ Recipes

KELSEY BARNARD CLARK

with Emily Heersink
Photographs by Antonis Achilleos

CHRONICLE BOOKS
SAN FRANCISCO

Text copyright © 2024 by Kelsey Barnard Clark.
Photographs copyright © 2024 by Antonis Achilleos.

Library of Congress Cataloging-in-Publication Data available.

ISBN 978-1-7972-2565-4

Manufactured in China.

Food styling by Kelsey Barnard Clark and team.
Prop styling assistance by Sarah Elizabeth Carroll.
Design by Lizzie Vaughan.
Typesetting by Wynne Au-Yeung.
Typeset in Chronicle Display, Chronicle Text, and Crossten.
Lettering of "Southern" by Jamar Cave.
Pattern by Lucy Engelman.

10 9 8 7 6 5 4 3 2 1

Chronicle books and gifts are available at special quantity discounts to
corporations, professional associations, literacy programs, and other
organizations. For details and discount information, please contact our
premiums department at corporatesales@chroniclebooks.com or at
1-800-759-0190.

Chronicle Books LLC
680 Second Street
San Francisco, California 94107
www.chroniclebooks.com

DEDICATION

This book is dedicated to my people—my phenomenal, cherished, fierce friends, of whom I have more than my fair share. Y'all are the best measures of my worth. Thank you for frequently filling my life and my home with laughter and joy, continuously inspiring me to set a loving table, and always giving me a reason to celebrate.

Getting Started
13

Daytime Delights
49

All-Day Bashes
97

Potlucks & Supper Clubs
153

Formal Affairs & Slow Food Socials
215

Introduction

There is a line in one of my favorite songs, "Crowded Table" by The Highwomen, which goes, "I want a house, with a crowded table." This song puts into words the feeling of comfort that comes from sharing a meal with those I love. Entertaining is my love language. I come alive at the thought of gathering friends or family around the table; of making a get-together feel special but never precious; of achieving a sense of ease, while always conveying the feeling that I went the extra mile. To me, celebrating friendship is as important as exercising a muscle. To celebrate my people continually, fervently, and joyfully through shared laughter and meals is to live fully.

Every good thing in life is a cause for celebration. I don't believe in keeping fine jewelry in boxes. Instead, I wear it all often, to add more joy and beauty to ordinary days (those who know me know this best). The same goes for the table. Don't save "the good stuff" for a special occasion. Life is too short and way too unpredictable. You never know when just an ordinary day will be one you'd give anything to go back and relive.

Southern Get-Togethers is the book I've always *really* wanted to write. It is the book I've been writing my entire life. This book is not just a cookbook; it's a go-to, one-stop shop for my biggest passions—gathering people to celebrate life and helping others feel empowered (not stressed) to do it too! The most important ingredient for a successful, fun party—the only thing that actually matters—is feeling happy and relaxed so that your guests follow suit. Have fun for God's sake! People might be impressed by fancy things, but what they will remember is how it felt to be there and how nice it was to be invited by *you*.

This book is a guide to real-life entertaining that comes from twenty years of hosting, both professionally and personally. I've made all the mistakes already and lived to tell the tale, and I want to give you the benefit of my experience so you can stop worrying and start celebrating. Think of this as your self-help manual for throwing the damn party. *Southern Get-Togethers* is applicable to any celebration and full of contingencies to help you gracefully navigate the unexpected. It's the encouragement you need to throw open your door and welcome the fun in. No fluff, no hired help, no exorbitant budgets—just attainable, work-with-what-you've-got, fabulous entertaining. After a global pandemic that left us craving connection and more aware than ever that there is no moment like the present, this is your guide to getting the party started!

PART

I

SOUTHERN GET-TOGETHERS

Getting Started

I'm sure you've heard that, when it comes to parties, it's all in the details. *Wrong!* It's not in the details, y'all. No one cares that you froze precious tiny roses in ice cubes, and they definitely do not care that you obsessively scrubbed every inch of your kitchen before they showed up. They care that you are present, calm, and inviting; that you are having fun and actually attending your own party. They care that they are well fed, well hydrated, and leave with nothing less—and nothing more— than the memory of time well spent. They care that you threw the party, and that they were invited. Screw the party favors you are obsessing over, the monogrammed napkins that didn't make it in time, and the over-the-top theme you didn't manage to pull off. Take it from the person who runs a catering company that has catered more than four hundred weddings and thousands of events: *No one* you care about cares.

A few years back, I catered the most luxurious, spare-no-expense, black-tie wedding, with caviar, sushi, ten food stations, and flowers dripping from every inch of the venue. Do you know what everyone lost their minds over and still bring up about that wedding? The McDonald's Happy Meals we tossed out on the dance floor during the last song.

So why am I starting off a book, a book on entertaining no less, by telling you this? Because this is a practical, you-can-do-this (anytime, anywhere, at any stage of life) type of book. This is a book to remind you that you should throw the damn party, every chance you get. No time to cook? Order takeout and throw the party. No money for florals? Clip those branches in your backyard (or visit someone else's) and throw the party. This is not the "proper" guide to setting the table, nor is it focused on the "right way" to do anything. It's about working with what you already have at home, gathering the ones you do life with, and creating memories that celebrate the everyday and the extraordinary.

Before we get to the recipes or even start to think about menu planning, there are some basic things to consider and ways to prepare for any party. This section includes my best of the best, rules of the trade, tried-and-true advice for setting yourself up for success— anywhere, anytime. Working a little hard on the front end ensures you are ready to host at a moment's notice. My main goal in writing this book is to encourage y'all to celebrate your life more, and then some. And this chapter is about setting you up to have the confidence to do just that.

The Prep
Building the Party-Ready Closet

I was in culinary school when I first heard the phrase "mise en place" or "everything in its place." At the time, it was just a term I had to learn. But now, it is the mantra of my life. Everything in its place—you included—or else everything is out of place. I'm not saying that everything has to look like a Pinterest board. I'm talking about the practical whereabouts of your things, a place for everything. Just as a stocked pantry is crucial in everyday cooking, a party closet is essential for easy entertaining. Here are the items I recommend keeping on hand.

Silverware. I suggest everyone have at least one 12-piece set each of salad forks, dinner forks, knives, and spoons. Additionally, I would invest in a dozen steak knives. Pick something neutral—silver or brass—that goes with everything. As someone who hosts large parties (twenty-plus guests) quite frequently, I have about six sets of silverware, and I am not afraid to mix and match when needed. You shouldn't be either! You do not need to break the bank on this, y'all. It doesn't need to be real silver or fancy—just something that isn't plastic and doesn't bend. That's it.

Cloth napkins & tablecloths. Two sets of a dozen napkins and two tablecloths are essential. Again, go neutral if this is all you have room for or are interested in keeping stocked. I love collecting table linens, so I have too many to admit to (bunnies for Easter, pumpkins for fall, etc.), but that's just my thing, and it is not necessary. Please, for the love of all things holy, do not buy expensive napkins or tablecloths. They will get candle wax on them. They will get beet juice and red wine stains on them. Do not waste your worry on linens, and do not be the host freaking out about the tablecloth. It ain't a good look.

Glassware. To be party ready, invest in a dozen of each: water, white wine, red wine, and rocks glasses. Choose a classic, clear, thick glass, with a stem, for all except the rocks glasses. Thin glass breaks too easily, and you'll be replacing these more often than you want. If you want to branch out, you, like me, might enjoy collecting antique glassware from local thrift stores. You can often find them for less than $1 per glass. I am a sucker for things I can thrift and collect—they always evoke a story and it's a fun hobby.

Dishware. White is the best decision here, y'all. It goes with everything and is appropriate for any meal. I recommend a dozen bread, salad, and dinner plates and a dozen bowls. You can never have enough platters. Stock a minimum of six to eight, of varying sizes and shapes, in white or clear glass. Another great option is to scour local antique stores or flea markets for silver platters. They add an instant fancy flair and can be purchased very affordably these days.

Chargers. We're not talking about the juice for your phones, y'all; we're talking about the large decorative plates that go underneath your dinner plates. I'm a fan of inexpensive cloth or rattan chargers. Chargers are another one

Place cards. I don't own any place cards, y'all. I prefer to use natural elements like beach pebbles, oyster shells, and fall leaves. All you need is a white or gold paint pen and your best handwriting (or someone else's) to turn a simple piece of nature into a pretty place card. Pro tip: Always write in cursive, even if you think it's messy. Print looks very elementary.

Flowers and candles. The more the merrier here. Flowers typically serve as the inspiration for my table, and I like to match my candles to them. Endless summer hydrangeas with candles in shades of lavender and blue, sunflowers with yellow candles, etc. Try it—it's a nice effect! When it comes to candleholders, I use classic clear glass holders, in varying heights, the most. Here are some rules of thumb for the number of candles needed for different size and shape tables:

- **Pillar candles:** six to eight candles (of varying heights) for a 6 to 8 ft [1.8 to 2.4 m] rectangular table or three to five candles for a 3 ft [0.9 m] round table

- **Tea candles:** eight tea candles for a 6 to 8 ft [1.8 to 2.4 m] rectangular table or five candles for a 3 ft [0.9 m] round table

Always have extra tea candles to warm up bathrooms, bars, or any dark corners.

of those things you can get crafty with if you enjoy it, and time allows. I've done moss, slates, or pizza stones in lieu of an actual charger. As with everything else, your go-to twelve chargers should be neutral, so you can dress up your table with other accents like florals, candles, and napkins.

Napkin rings. I typically coordinate my napkin rings with my silverware or chargers. My everyday rings are hammered silver, antique brass, and rattan. Like table linens, there are endless opportunities to add to your collection if you choose—leaves for fall, crowns for Mardi Gras, etc. They are inexpensive and easy to find. Remember that whatever you plan to use as your everyday rings should coordinate with your other everyday tableware, just as your favorite belt or everyday jewelry goes with just about everything.

The Prep
Building the Party-Ready Pantry

The beauty of a fully stocked pantry (and I use that term loosely to include your refrigerator and freezer too) is that it allows you to host events on the fly. These impromptu get-togethers don't have to be fancy, and the food doesn't have to be homemade—it just has to be there, ready to eat. Look, I get that last-minute gatherings can seem especially stressful, but I swear, if you keep your kitchen stocked with these staples, you *will* be able to host a delicious, spur-of-the-moment hang—and you won't ever regret the time spent with your nearest and dearest. These are the tried-and-true items I keep on hand, so I'm always prepared for some laid-back, easy entertaining. After all, snacks are the most important meal of the day.

DRIED/JARRED/CANNED

- [ ] Chili crunch (my favorite brands are This Little Goat, Momofuku, Lao Gan Ma, and Fly by Jing)
- [ ] Crackers
- [ ] Dipping sauces for bread (aged balsamic vinegar, herbed olive oil, and olive tapenade)
- [ ] Everything bagel seasoning
- [ ] Jarred tomato sauce (Rao's is my fave)
- [ ] Marinated artichoke hearts
- [ ] Marinated mushrooms
- [ ] Minced garlic
- [ ] Nuts
- [ ] Parmesan cheese crisps
- [ ] Pickled gherkins, green beans, okra, and peppers
- [ ] Pita
- [ ] Popcorn (pick your favorite flavor, but I like kettle corn for hosting)
- [ ] Pork rinds
- [ ] Ramen noodles
- [ ] Whole stewed tomatoes

FROZEN

- [ ] Dumplings, egg rolls, pot stickers, or spring rolls
- [ ] Edamame
- [ ] French bread loaves
- [ ] Fresh sliced mozzarella
- [ ] Pesto
- [ ] Pizza dough
- [ ] Prosciutto

REFRIGERATED

- [ ] Bruschetta topping
- [ ] Gyoza dipping sauce
- [ ] Homemade marinated olives
- [ ] Hummus
- [ ] 1 to 2 varieties each of hard and soft cheeses
- [ ] Parmesan cheese
- [ ] Pimiento cheese
- [ ] Ponzu sauce

The Prep
Building the Party-Ready Bar

If you have these bar ingredients stocked, you'll be able to whip
up a variety of classic cocktails or mocktails, and then some!

LIQUORS

- [ ] Aperol
- [ ] Blanco tequila
- [ ] Bourbon
- [ ] Dark rum
- [ ] Dry vermouth
- [ ] Gin
- [ ] Reposado tequila
- [ ] St-Germain elderflower liqueur
- [ ] Vodka

MIXERS

- [ ] Bitters
- [ ] Coconut milk
- [ ] Ginger beer
- [ ] Orange blossom syrup
- [ ] Orange juice (canned lasts forever)
- [ ] Simple syrup
- [ ] Soda water
- [ ] Sugar cubes
- [ ] Tonic water

GARNISHES

- [ ] Lemons
- [ ] Limes
- [ ] Mint leaves
- [ ] Olives
- [ ] Oranges
- [ ] Preserved cherries

The Who, Why, When, and Where

I am a planner. I like charts, foolproof calculations, outlines, and lists. But honestly, when it comes to hosting, four simple questions go the furthest in setting you up for success. Ask yourself these questions before you start to organize any party, and use your responses as a road map throughout the planning process.

Who? Who are you inviting to this event? What are the age groups and what does that mean? What type of relationship do you have with your guests? Answering these simple questions will guide you to choose either a more casual or a more formal event. For example, if kids are invited, then the event will be more casual, while an older crowd may lead you toward a more formal event. Having your boss over for dinner versus your best friend being in town are obviously two very different types of gatherings. Plan the menu and seating around who you're hosting.

Why? Why are you gathering? Are your intentions to talk business, recruit a client, or simply to have fun? What do you believe your guests expect from this gathering? If I'm getting girlfriends together to catch up, I'm going straight to my Potlucks & Supper Clubs chapter (see page 153) for casual ease, while the Formal Affairs & Slow Food Socials chapter (see page 215) offers the sit-down menus meant to impress a special guest.

When? When is this gathering taking place? A 4 to 6 p.m. gathering is going to have a completely different feel than a 6 to 8 p.m. event. In the afternoon, snacks are totally acceptable and appreciated, but in the evening, a meal is expected. The time of day you host influences how and what to serve.

Where? Where is this event taking place? Indoors or outdoors? A full barbecue spread on bamboo or themed plates is typically appropriate for boot-clad backyard or barn fetes but not for a cocktail party. Take your venue and weather into account when planning and make adjustments as needed!

The Table

Alright y'all, let me make this perfectly clear: The following table setting formulas are not "the right way" to set a table according to any official guides. This is my practical, more modern approach to setting a table: a version where coffee typically isn't consumed at the end of the meal, and we can probably just use one wine glass for whatever we are drinking. It's table setting whittled down to what is necessary and 100 percent will be used.

Formal OCCASIONS

Glassware: Water glass, champagne flute, all-purpose wine glass

Silverware: Salad and dinner fork, salad and dinner or steak knife, soup or dessert spoon, if needed

Napkins: Folded with a ring, or folded into a rectangle under the plate

Plates: Salad, dinner, and dessert plate; bread and butter plate; charger

Semiformal OCCASIONS

Glassware: Water glass, all-purpose wine glass

Silverware: Salad and dinner fork, salad and dinner or steak knife, soup or dessert spoon, if needed

Napkins: Folded with a ring, folded into a rectangle under the plate, or folded into a rectangle with silverware on top

Plates: Salad, dinner, and dessert plate; charger

Casual DINNER

Glassware: Water glass

Silverware: Dinner fork and dinner or steak knife, spoon only if needed for soup or dessert (This setting is meant to be family style–esque; guests use the same silverware and plates for all courses.)

Napkins: Folded with a ring or folded into a rectangle under the plate

Plates: Dinner plate, charger

Potluck OR *Buffet*

Glassware: Rocks, wine, and champagne glasses, as well as cocktail napkins, set up at a bar area for guests to serve themselves. Setting out some cut citrus, an ice bucket, and cocktail stirrers is always a nice gesture.

Silverware: Silverware, grouped by function, in a jar, pitcher, or bowl, alongside the stacked plates

Napkins: Folded and stacked, beside the stacked plates

Plates: Plates stacked at the beginning of the buffet/potluck line

Serveware: For potlucks, I always ask guests to bring dishes in white, silver, or glass (everyone has one of these) to ensure the spread is cohesive. I have a no–slow cooker rule for appearance reasons, as well as the fact that tripping over a cord is less than ideal with a plate of food in your hand. Don't forget to put out serving spoons! Most guests will not bring these with their potluck dish.

The Florals

At fifteen, I began my career as a culinary assistant working for Larry, owner of Larry Paul Catering and Flowers. I was in it purely for the catering experience, but I'm so thankful for my time watching Larry create floral magic. Two decades later, arranging flowers remains one of my favorite forms of therapy. My approach to arranging is admittedly untrained, but playing with nature and creating beauty with my hands is a great joy. There's still a child inside each of us, and a walk in the woods, your yard, or your neighborhood can serve as the greatest treasure hunt of all if you let it. I urge y'all to have fun doing this and to find your own way, as I think we get the most from flower arranging when we experiment. But if you want a place to start, here are a few tips and a little peek into my process.

Tip One
COLLECT YOUR TOOLS

This is a basic list of what I use 90 percent of the time to throw together a centerpiece (or five!) for a get-together:

- Chicken wire
- Floral scissors
- Floral tape
- Glass cleaner
- Goo Gone adhesive remover
- Green Glo plant polish spray
- Pruning shears
- Spanish moss and sheet moss
- Spray bottle

Tip Two

PREP YOUR VESSELS

Start a collection. Over time, personalize your vessel collection with unique items: treasures found in the back of closets, chipped urns on sale at flea markets, or your grandmother's forgotten silver. China coffee urns, gravy boats, and ice buckets all work well. I rarely use vessels that are meant to hold flowers—and that is the fun of it!

Consider placement. When choosing which vessel to use for an arrangement, consider where you'll place it first. For a centerpiece, sit at the table to get a feel for the ideal size and height for your flowers—you want people to be able to see each other during a meal.

Clean your vessel. If using glass or crystal, spray the inside with glass cleaner, then rinse thoroughly for a crystal-clear appearance.

Stop the flop. A lot of florists use floral foam to provide structure for an arrangement, but I'm not a fan of that approach. It is messy, expensive, harmful for the environment and aquatic life, and prevents flowers from drinking straight from fresh water, which causes them to die faster. Instead, I use rice, pebbles, chicken wire, or floral tape. (Keep in mind that rice swells in water, so don't add too much.) Chicken wire can be cut in the shape of the container's opening and taped to the sides. For a similar effect, I use floral or electrical tape to create a tic-tac-toe grid over the mouth of the container (see photo). All of these methods provide a great base for arranging stems.

Tip Three

PREP YOUR FLOWERS

Trim the stems. Whether you are buying or picking your own flowers, always cut them fresh on the diagonal and immediately place them in water. Trimming the stems on the bias gives them more surface area from which to drink.

Cut in the morning. If you are cutting fresh flowers, always cut them in the morning or evening, and never in the heat of the day, which will cause flowers to wilt or die almost instantaneously.

Always strip your stems. Leaves that are left submerged in water will result in murky, smelly "fish tank" water, which also causes flowers to die more quickly. I simply pull the leaves off with my hands and then use an old sponge to strip the stems. I find this is the best way to protect flowers, as well as delicate, softer stems such as tulips.

Clean off pollen. Remove visible, dark pollen from flowers like lilies and amaryllis. These stain the flowers yellow, and will shed and stain anything they touch. Gently squeeze the pollen at the tip of the anthers (threads covered with pollen in the center of flowers) and pull. If some of the yellow pollen drops on the petals, dust it and then spray with water to wash it away.

Spritz often. I keep a spray bottle filled with water handy at all times and spritz flowers right after cutting, as many drink from their petals as well as their stems.

Tip Four
CONSIDER THE BASICS

Plan around the occasion. Start by picking either a color palette or theme, such as a specific holiday, for your table setting or buffet. Whatever you choose to be the guide, stick to it. Think of your table like an outfit and plan your accessories (i.e., flowers) accordingly. I tend to pick one, maybe two, colors and use those colors in varying shades with pops of green and white.

Add texture via greenery! Unless I am doing bud vases with delicate tulips, dahlias, or poppies, I include greenery in my arrangements. I like to use a minimum of three different types of greenery, and sometimes up to five. When picking greenery, I look for stems in varying lengths and leaves in different shapes and colors. I never buy greenery and instead opt to use what I can cut from outside (which I understand is not always possible depending on where you live). This not only cuts costs, but it also gives a seasonal feel to any arrangement. My favorite greenery clippings are magnolia, boxwood, podocarp, ferns, ivy, palms, and anything with berries. I'm also a big fan of incorporating fresh herbs like rosemary, oregano, bolted basil, chive flowers, and parsley.

Keep it wild. Arrangements that look like a tight ball look just that—tight. No one likes a tight wad, y'all. Keep it looking loose and wild by making sure your arrangement has varying heights. If you find an arrangement looks too scrunched, simply pull a few pieces of greenery or flowers out, creating a drooping, wisteria-like effect.

Flowers are like good friends; they travel in groups. When using bud vases, I include a minimum of three, but typically five, in varying heights. In lieu of one large arrangement, I often use three smaller containers in varying sizes, filled with arrangements that use similar colors and textures. Remember: Odd numbers are the name of the game.

Tip Five
CHANGE THE WATER

Keep it fresh. Once you've created your arrangement, change the water every day or two. This will keep your arrangement fresh for as long as possible.

The Mind of a Chef
How to Plan Any Menu, Anytime

Planning a menu is of the utmost importance to a chef. It's a studied practice that comes with time, experience, and repetition. For a home cook, here is my advice for planning menus.

Expand your library. First, buy *The New Food Lover's Companion* by Sharon Tyler Herbst and Ron Herbst and *The Flavor Bible* by Andrew Dornenburg and Karen Page. Both books are what young chefs use to understand which flavors and ingredients go well together, and which don't. These books were instrumental in my training years, and I still reference them.

Know the five commandments of taste: salt, fat, acid, heat, texture. Most dishes should contain all of these elements, or if a single dish doesn't, the meal as a whole definitely should. How will you know? Taste your food. Salt is typically the easiest to decipher. Fat is sneaky. It doesn't just mean oil. Fat imparts velvety notes and can come in many forms, such as avocado, cheese, yogurt, stock, and, of course, butter. When you taste your food, is it a little flat or lacking in something you can't quite put your finger on? That missing something is almost always acid. Give the dish a good squeeze of lemon or add a tomato, a pickle, or a splash of vinegar (or even honey, a balance enabler), and you may be surprised by how much this wakes it up. When I say heat, I don't mean physical heat. I mean an ingredient that gives the dish a little bite. This can be something as small as a crack of black pepper, a handful of arugula, or a sprinkle of fresh herbs. And finally, texture. I can hardly think of a dish that isn't made better with a little crunch—think croutons, raw vegetables and fruits, nuts, or a fried garnish. Keep these elements in mind when it comes to planning your menu. Don't serve meat and three sides that are all variations of veggies with cream (think mashed potatoes, potato gratin, sweet potato casserole). Instead, give your menu variety, introduce an element of acid (a salad with a tart vinaigrette), make sure there is texture (crunchy green beans), fat (avocado, olive oil), adjust the spice, and season with salt to give each dish balance.

Consider the presentation. Most chefs plan every element of a dish, including how it will look on the table, long before it ever hits the plate. When it comes to cooking at home, this means taking a minute to think about how you will serve your food. For example, if you're setting up a buffet, a row of six foil casserole dishes just isn't appealing. Do your best to avoid disposable plastic serveware. It doesn't have to be fancy—simple glass or white pieces work just fine.

The Charts

After a few years of catering events, I came up with these charts to determine how much food and drink you need for any party. They were developed from analyzing, testing, and tracking real-life events of every kind, and their success rate is right up there with birth control. They're extensive, precise, thoughtful, based on experience, and should be followed to a freakin' T. Say goodbye to recurring worries about having enough food, drinks, or ice. I've got you covered.

This right here is the KBC bible that we've been using since 2012 for predicting consumption at a party, and now that I think of it, *I can't believe I am putting this in a book!* Ok, enjoy (and don't second-guess this).

BAR NOTES

This chart is not suggesting that your guests will consume this much alcohol; I am not promoting irresponsibility. But you don't know what guests will drink more or less of, so you want to have more than enough. Your guests should know their limit and drink responsibly. And they should not drink and drive. OK, done being the mom.

Red vs. white vs. sparkling wine is totally dependent on your crowd. I know my group of girlfriends are big bubbles drinkers, but this isn't always the case. Up the white wine in Spring/Summer and the red in Fall/Winter.

BAR

BASED ON A 4- TO 5-HOUR EVENT	10 PEOPLE	20 PEOPLE	50 PEOPLE	100 PEOPLE	150 PEOPLE
Beer and Wine Bar · 40% beer, 60% wine					
Beer bottles (12 oz/350 ml)	18	37	75	150	225
Wine bottles (25 oz/750 ml)	14	28	56	112	168
Beer, Wine, and Liquor Bar · 20% beer, 50% wine, 30% liquor					
Beer bottles (12 oz/350 ml)	15	30	60	120	180
Wine bottles (25 oz/750 ml)	9	19	38	76	114
Liquor Tequila, vodka, and whiskey/bourbon are standard	1 fifth (25 oz/750 ml) of each desired type of liquor	1 fifth (25 oz/750 ml) of each desired type of liquor	1 liter (34 oz) of each desired type of liquor	10 handles (60 oz/1.75 L) of desired types of liquor	15 handles (60 oz/1.75 L) of desired types of liquor
Mixers · 1 quart (945 ml) per 3 people					
Coke, Diet Coke, soda, tonic, juices	4	8	17	34	51
Ice	2.5 lbs [1 kg] per person always				

FOOD

Plated · 1 protein + 2 sides	
Protein	6 to 8 oz [170 to 230 g] per person
Veggies	4 to 6 oz [115 to 170 g] per person
Starch	4 to 6 oz [115 to 170 g] per person
Buffet · 2 or 3 proteins + 4 sides	
Protein	4 oz [115 g] per person for each protein
Veggies	4 oz [115 g] per person for each veggie
Starch	4 oz [115 g] per person for each starch
Passed Appetizers	
Always 2 or 3 bites or pieces per person (if serving 2 or 3 apps, 3 of each per person; if serving 3 to 5 apps, 2 of each per person)	

Hosting Guidelines

This is all about reading the room, y'all. I am not a therapist, psychologist, or psychiatrist. However, after nearly twenty years in this hospitality business, I can typically predict when a dinner may turn sour (and we're not talking about the food). Here are a few things to consider when hosting to ensure everyone feels comfortable and your event goes smoothly.

Be food appropriate. I love ribs; in the South, we all love ribs. But when you're hosting your boss for dinner, serving ribs is probably not the best idea. Messy, fun food is for your messy, fun friends. Stick to traditional, fork and knife–type meals for more formal or serious guests.

Be communicative. If you want your guests to bring their own alcohol, leave their kids/dog/mom/partner at home, whatever—tell them. Getting mad or harboring resentment that "Bob" always mooches is probably on you. Boundaries are key and setting them is important. Here's how you do this: "Hey! Would love to have you and Sarah over Saturday. Drinks at 5 p.m., dinner around 6 p.m. Please BYOB—we've got the food covered. Adults and humans only. Hope you can make it!"

Be timely. When hosting, food should be served no later than one to one and a half hours after guests arrive (i.e., drinks at five, dinner at six). Don't be the host who has kids screaming and guests snapping because they are literally starving and/or ready to go home.

Be thoughtful about the menu. I'm talking about dietary restrictions here. As a host, ask if anyone has a *serious* aversion or allergy and avoid it. Someone "not liking onions" does not apply here. Likewise, if you, as the host, are on a keto or fat-free diet, having only restricted food options on your menu is not the most thoughtful approach. Of course, both hosts and guests should be reasonable. If I'm attending dinner at the home of a vegetarian friend, I expect a meatless meal, but if I'm attending dinner at the home of a friend who follows all the fad diets, I better not have to suffer through a sodium-, fat-, protein-, and starch-free meal. Get it?

Be culturally appropriate. Guys, I need y'all to listen to me. Please do not attempt to make a "culturally appropriate" meal from the culture you think your neighbor is a part of. I've heard versions of this scenario so many times and I'll never not cringe. Where exactly is your neighbor from? Oh, you don't know? You're not 100 percent sure, or even 50 percent sure? Right. The chances that you will nail the food of a country or culture you are not even certain you're familiar with are slim to none. The chances of butchering the dish, creating an awkward situation, and possibly offending are high. There's a lesson to remember here: Take into account any dietary restrictions (see "Be thoughtful about the menu"), and then stick to what you cook best when having new people over. My meal is Roast Chicken (page 222). It's a simple crowd-pleaser and a great no-stress meal when I need to focus on getting to know my guests.

The Social Reminders
Mind Your P's and Q's but Break Some Rules

Manners and etiquette are as embedded in Southern culture as sweet tea and Sunday church, but I am the first to chuck the rules that are past their prime (and there are plenty!). I've broken this down really simply for you as a host or as a guest. So here they are: ten traditional, long-standing rules for being a good host and a good guest, and whether or not you should *trash* them because they're dated or *keep* them because they still hold up.

FOR THE HOST

Trash. **Don't talk about sex, politics, or religion.** But proceed with caution. If you are unwilling to discuss said topics without being open, respectful, and willing to listen to others' opinions, then this is a hard no. Similarly, if you are inviting someone who you believe is unwilling to discuss said topics without being open, respectful, and willing to listen to others' opinions, then this is a hard no. What I mean to say is: Know your crowd before bringing up these topics. And know how to change the subject if things get dodgy. For example, I love discussing current hot topics with my group of girlfriends. Why? Because I know it will be a fulfilling, challenging conversation grounded in curiosity and respect. I also know it will be convivial because I know my audience. I am not having that conversation with anyone I don't know well or fear may not be cordial. Sticky subjects can be discussed with people you know like glue. Got it?

Keep. **Always set the table.** The table doesn't have to be fancy. It can be casual and thrown together, but having it set before people arrive

is one of those things that makes your guests feel special, welcome, and wanted.

Keep. **Always make extras.** I want my home to have an open door, and that means always having more than enough food. Making a few extra servings is an easy way to lower stress and drama. For me, it's always three extra servings (OK, it's more like five to ten, but that's overdoing it, y'all; don't be me).

Keep. **Always have fresh flowers on the table.** I'm not talking about peonies and poppies flown in for dinner in January. I'm talking about bringing the outside in, y'all! There is something so relaxed, beautiful, and thoughtful when you walk into a home infused with the season's gifts. Even in the middle of winter in New York. Nude branches in a glass vase are dramatic, modern even. There is always a plethora of life outside—bring it into your home.

Trash. **Always have prepared hors d'oeuvres upon arrival.** In a pinch, I once set out a bowl of my kids' cheese puffs that ended up sparking

40

such happy, nostalgic conversation among guests while they dipped their orange-coated fingers back in the bowl faster than I could keep it filled. It's nice if you have time, but it's not something to stress about.

Trash. **Always have a pressed hand towel in the powder room.** Don't run the wash for this. Don't worry about the monogram. If you have a pristine towel, great, but it's gonna be crumpled up after the first guest uses it regardless.

Keep. **Always save the dirty dishes for later.** First off, I want my guests to enjoy their time, and I want to enjoy them up until the last call. Secondly, I don't want someone doing my dishes. Too many glasses get broken this way, fine china gets ruined in the dishwasher, cast iron gets soaked—you get the drill. Micromanaging the volunteer dishwasher makes for a sour end to a good night.

Trash. **Always direct guests and give a toast before the meal.** Just because you are the host doesn't mean everyone needs to hear your voice all night. One of my biggest pet peeves is when I go to a dinner and the host acts like he's a train conductor all night. "Let me get your attention real quick," dings glass, "bathrooms are this way." Dings glass again, "Since we are

an hour into the party, let me explain where everyone needs to sit." Dings glass, once again, "Now that everyone is seated, I'd like to thank all of you for being here" (and talk about myself for five minutes). This constant direction is an interruption to the flow of conversation among guests and what could otherwise be a wonderful gathering. You know you've encountered one of these hosts; don't even think about lying to me.

Keep. **Always have a pitcher of something on hand.** There are no real rules here, y'all. From "I've got a pot of coffee on," to "Let me get you a glass of punch," having a beverage prepared ahead of time to offer guests is a welcoming gesture and makes a gracious first impression. What's more, a pitcher of a mixed cocktail or drinks set out ahead of time keeps things simple, and it can prevent your whole bar from getting drained.

Keep. **Always have music on and candles lit.** Music is the best cure for awkward silence, and it absolutely sets the tone. I often have guests play DJ on the record player or sound system as a fun icebreaker. Music is a universal language, after all. Candles or diffusers are an easy, homey touch. And there's no work involved—just light them fifteen minutes before guests arrive.

FOR THE GUEST

Keep. **Don't assume you have a plus-one (or two or three or four).** I love having an open door and a home where everyone feels welcome. But I also love to be prepared. If it's not clear who is invited, ask! This allows the host to give you an answer and prepare accordingly.

Keep. **Always bring a bottle of something you enjoy drinking.** This rule kills two birds with one stone. While I don't ever want my guests to feel obligated to bring a hostess gift, it's always a good idea to make a gesture of contribution to the bar or table. It's the host's call whether

to open it for the occasion, but it increases the chances you'll have something you like to quench your thirst.

Keep. **Always be respectful when you are in someone's home.** Ask where you should put your bag and coat; don't just throw them on the nearest surface. Keep your feet off the furniture, pillows off the ground, and kids off literally everything except the grass and kid-designated areas. And speaking of kid-designated areas, be sure they aren't destroying said area. "Kid-designated" does not mean let the kids stomp on Goldfish crackers, throw toys everywhere, and draw on the walls. The best rule of thumb for kids' behavior? Expect your child to behave as they do in the classroom at school. Also: Ask the host if there are any house rules (like no shoes inside) and make sure your child hears them and that you enforce them.

Keep. **Be punctual, but never early.** Y'all, no host wants you to come early to help. They just don't. In my case, the last thirty minutes before the party is when I indulge in my pre-party, mood-enhancing ritual. I lock the bathroom door and watch *Sex and the City*, with a glass of champagne, while I put a gloss coat on my nails. This is my sacred "party game face" routine; please do not ruin it by ringing the bell early. If you come early on a day when I didn't leave enough time for my favorite ritual, it will be even worse. You may walk into a throw down fight about *someone* deciding to blow off the patio, again, despite the pristinely laid table on said patio. You know, just hypothetically. Don't come early. As a guest, fashionably late is thirty minutes, not an hour. And don't be the guest who always arrives late or overstays their welcome either—overstaying is anything past four to five hours (i.e., arrive at five, get the F outta there by ten at the absolute latest).

Keep. **Always offer to help.** Ask, but do not ask more than once. And don't do it anyway, when the host clearly stated that they do not need help. See a frantic, frazzled host on the verge of tears? Quietly ask if they'd like a drink and whisper that you're happy to take a breather out back if they'd like. Do not make it a scene. Asking if you can help is courteous; pestering to help is bothersome. Listen and respect boundaries.

Keep. **Ignore the phone.** Y'all, I am not always the best at this, but I'm trying to be better. It's distracting to have a guest who's taking calls, checking emails, or scrolling through social media and only half listening to conversations all night. While so many of us do this reflexively and mean no harm, it sends the message that the people you are with are less important than your phone. I'm not saying to leave your phone in the car. As a mother of two young kids, I'm always going to keep my phone close by, but there are ways to let it take a backseat, such as setting a separate ringtone for the babysitter or a friend in crisis and otherwise not touching it.

Keep. **Avoid shop talk.** If the host wants to talk about your new business idea, invention, or investing in either, they will bring it up, or invite you to a business lunch or a meeting. Bombarding a host with your personal agenda is not a good look.

Keep. **Don't hog the host (or fellow guests).** No one likes to be stuck in a conversation with a single person all night. The point of a party is varied conversation with multiple people. It is not a date, interview, or counseling session.

Keep. **Be mindful of food portions.** I'm talking about serve-yourself or buffet-style parties here. If you know that there are five people behind you and there are six baked potatoes left, don't take two of them. This is first grade math, y'all. Help a host out.

Trash. **Make a strong first impression.** Instead, make a daily, nightly, frequent impression with your candid conversation, witty banter, and bright personality. The number of times I've changed my mind after a first impression is too many to count. Mistakes will be made, and things will be said that you wish could be unsaid. 'Tis life. Don't sweat it.

PART

II

SOUTHERN GET-TOGETHERS

Daytime Delights

Daytime hosting is often overlooked in favor of evening affairs, but I love a daytime gathering. It doesn't carry the pressure of the last meal of the day; the food tends to be more casual; your guests are thankful to have enjoyed something outside of the routine; and it's especially great for multigenerational groups. Hosting in the daytime also means you can prepare the night before and cleanup is done in time for there to be a second act to the day. These brunch and lunch menus are flexible, uncomplicated, and can be dressed up or down. If you feel daunted by preparing an impressive formal dinner, don't! Instead, throw together a pantry cheeseboard, send out a quick BYOB text, and invite a few friends to enjoy these daytime delights!

Foolproof
Joint Hosting

Returning to live in the small town where I grew up means I have a group of friends that spans decades. From the high school graduation parties thrown by our parents to the baby showers we host now, this group of women has learned by doing. Now that we've hit our entertaining stride, we have a foolproof recipe for jointly hosting the perfect formal brunch or luncheon to celebrate life's milestones. Given the inclusive guest list and the big life events these parties commemorate, some extra planning for these get-togethers goes a long way to ensure their success.

When planning a celebration hosted by a group, it's crucial to designate a house host and a lead host. These could be the same person, but not necessarily. The lead host is the person who will create the "to do" list, delegate tasks, set the budget, enforce the budget, serve as point person for questions, and be the final say for whatever decisions might need to be made while planning, thereby avoiding the incessant text chain of indecisiveness. As lead host, delegating and communicating are top priorities. Delegating is not dictating. Delegating is playing matchmaker between tasks and volunteers. In my experience, communicating clearly ahead of time is the key to a fun and flawless event. For larger, more formal events, you'll never regret the extra time you put into the prep.

LEAD HOST CHECKLIST

- ☐ Create invitations and send them by the deadline; budget for paper and postage if mailing invitations.

- ☐ Communicate with the guest of honor about the guest list, keep track of RSVPs, follow up with guests who have not responded, and provide an accurate head count one week ahead of the event.

- ☐ Ask every cohost to bring a dish; ensure there is enough food for the size of the gathering and duplicate dishes only when needed.

- ☐ Provide ice and any nonalcoholic hot or cold beverages and serving containers. Feel free to delegate this.

- ☐ Provide alcohol if serving, along with any mixers and garnishes. Feel free to delegate this. Be sure to check my chart (see page 37) for quantities and varieties to create an accurate list for both alcoholic and nonalcoholic beverages.

HOUSE HOST CHECKLIST

- ☐ Provide the plates, silverware, and glasses.

- ☐ Provide extra serving pieces for cohosts who forget to bring them. To minimize the need for additional serving pieces, ask cohosts to bring their dishes in white, silver or glass (no chafing dishes or slow cookers). This creates a more uniform, pleasing table.

- ☐ Set the table and manage the florals. If you aren't doing the florals yourself, inventory how many arrangements you will need based on where they will go in your home.

- ☐ Communicate when other cohosts should arrive to help on the day of the event.

- ☐ Delegate any other tasks related to hosting the party at your home. This could include arranging the florals, bringing ironed table linens, providing additional glassware, or designing place cards, menus, and signage. Don't assume others will chip in and don't be shy—ask for help where you want it (this goes for life as well as hosting!).

THE BEST BRUNCH MENU

This is my go-to menu for morning or midday hosting. A frittata is perfect for both planned celebrations and impromptu, cook-what-you've-got get-togethers. The three variations that follow are my favorites, but the beauty of a frittata is that you can load it with whatever veggies, cheeses, and other savory bits and bobs you have leftover in the refrigerator.

For a sit-down celebration— if you're throwing a graduation, baptism, or birthday brunch, for example—round out the meal with the Spinach and Frisée Salad and Berry Clafoutis. Both recipes are French inspired. The tart vinegar, crisp lettuce, and smoky bacon in this simple, classic salad complement the frittata so well. A clafoutis (technically a French breakfast pastry) is such a delight and easy to execute. While it shines for breakfast, it can also be sliced and served with a dollop of whipped cream for dessert. At brunch, you get the best of both worlds! The salad and the clafoutis can both be made ahead, which helps make hosting a snap.

Frittata, Three Ways

SERVES 4 TO 6

8 large eggs

½ cup [120 ml] heavy cream or whole milk

1 cup [140 g] diced onion

1 Tbsp kosher salt

8 to 10 turns freshly ground black pepper

Add-ins (recipes follow)

2 Tbsp olive oil or unsalted butter

In a medium bowl, beat the eggs. Add the heavy cream or milk, onion, salt, and pepper and mix to combine. Add add-ins for any frittata version you desire (variations follow).

Set the broiler to high.

In a medium skillet over medium-high heat, warm the olive oil or butter. Drop a bit of egg mixture into the pan and if it sizzles, the pan is ready. Pour the egg mixture into the skillet, scraping the bowl with a rubber spatula. Swirl the pan to distribute the egg mixture evenly. Shake the pan gently, tilting it slightly with one hand while lifting the edges of the frittata with a spatula in your other hand to let the eggs run underneath during the first few minutes of cooking. Once a few layers of egg have cooked, turn the heat to low, cover (use a pizza pan if you don't have a lid that fits your skillet), and cook for 10 minutes, occasionally shaking the pan gently. Uncover the pan and place it under the broiler for 1 to 2 minutes, or until the top is golden and set. Cool for at least 5 minutes. Cut into wedges and serve. Store leftovers wrapped tightly in plastic wrap in the refrigerator for up to 3 days.

No. One

Mushroom, Goat Cheese, and Spinach Frittata

1 Tbsp olive oil

2 cups [120 g] sliced mushrooms
(I love wild, but get whatever looks good to you)

4 cups [80 g] packed baby spinach

1 cup [200 g] chopped tomatoes

4 oz [115 g] goat cheese, crumbled

1 bunch fresh basil, leaves finely chopped

1 tsp dried oregano

In a medium sauté pan over high heat, warm the olive oil. Add the mushrooms and sear for about 4 minutes, flipping halfway through cooking, or until slightly crispy and golden. Add the mushrooms, along with the spinach, tomatoes, goat cheese, basil, and oregano to the frittata base and cook the frittata as directed (see page 56).

No. Two

Tomato, Prosciutto, and Mozzarella Frittata

2 cups [400 g] chopped tomatoes

4 to 6 oz [115 to 170 g] prosciutto
or cooked bacon, chopped

2 cups [160 g] shredded mozzarella

Add the tomatoes, prosciutto or bacon, and mozzarella to the frittata base and cook the frittata as directed (see page 56).

No. Three

Summer Squash and Gruyère Frittata

4 cups [320 g] zucchini and squash noodles

1 tsp kosher salt

8 oz [230 g] grated Gruyère cheese

⅛ tsp red pepper flakes

2 oz [55 g] grated Parmesan cheese

¼ cup [15 g] panko

In a large bowl, toss the zucchini and squash noodles with the salt. Let stand at room temperature for at least 20 minutes and up to 2 hours. Drain the noodles, pressing with your hands to squeeze out as much liquid as possible.

Add the zucchini and squash noodles, Gruyère, and red pepper flakes to the frittata base. Cook the frittata as directed on the stove, then sprinkle with the Parmesan and panko and finish cooking under the broiler (see page 56).

Spinach and Frisée Salad

SERVES 4 TO 6

6 bacon slices, chopped

1 shallot, finely diced

¼ cup [60 ml] red wine vinegar

1 Tbsp honey

8 cups [160 g] packed baby spinach, frisée, or arugula

1 bunch fresh chives, chopped

¼ cup [25 g] shaved pecorino romano cheese
or ¼ cup [20 g] Parmesan cheese

2 Tbsp olive oil

Kosher salt

Freshly ground black pepper

In a medium skillet or sauté pan over medium heat, cook the bacon for 5 to 8 minutes, or until it's crispy and the fat has rendered. Add the shallot and cook until translucent, about 3 minutes. Remove from the heat and add the vinegar and honey, stirring to scrape up all the bacon bits from the pan.

In a large bowl, combine the spinach, frisée, chives, pecorino romano or Parmesan, olive oil, and a pinch of salt and pepper. Add the bacon dressing and toss well. Season with salt and pepper to taste. Serve immediately.

Berry Clafoutis

SERVES 6 TO 8

2 cups [240 g] berries

Zest of 1 lemon

Zest of 1 orange

1 cup [200 g] granulated sugar

1 cup [140 g] all-purpose flour

1 cup [240 ml] whole milk

3 large eggs

2 Tbsp unsalted butter, at room temperature

1 Tbsp vanilla extract

⅛ tsp kosher salt

Confectioners' sugar, for dusting

Preheat the oven to 350°F [180°C]. Lightly butter a 9 by 13 in [23 by 33 cm] baking dish at least 1½ in [4 cm] deep.

In a medium mixing bowl, toss together the berries and zests, then set aside.

In a food processor, blender, or large bowl with an immersion blender, combine the granulated sugar, flour, milk, eggs, butter, vanilla, and salt. Blend on high speed until smooth and frothy, about 1 minute.

Pour a ½ in [13 mm] layer of batter into the prepared baking dish. Bake for about 15 minutes, or until the batter just barely sets. Remove from the oven, add the berries in a single layer, and pour in the remaining batter. Bake for 1 hour, or until the batter is completely cooked and the edges are slightly firm and golden. A knife inserted into the middle should come out clean. Remove from the oven and let cool for 5 minutes. Dust with confectioners' sugar and serve warm or at room temperature. Place in an airtight container and store in the refrigerator for up to 3 days.

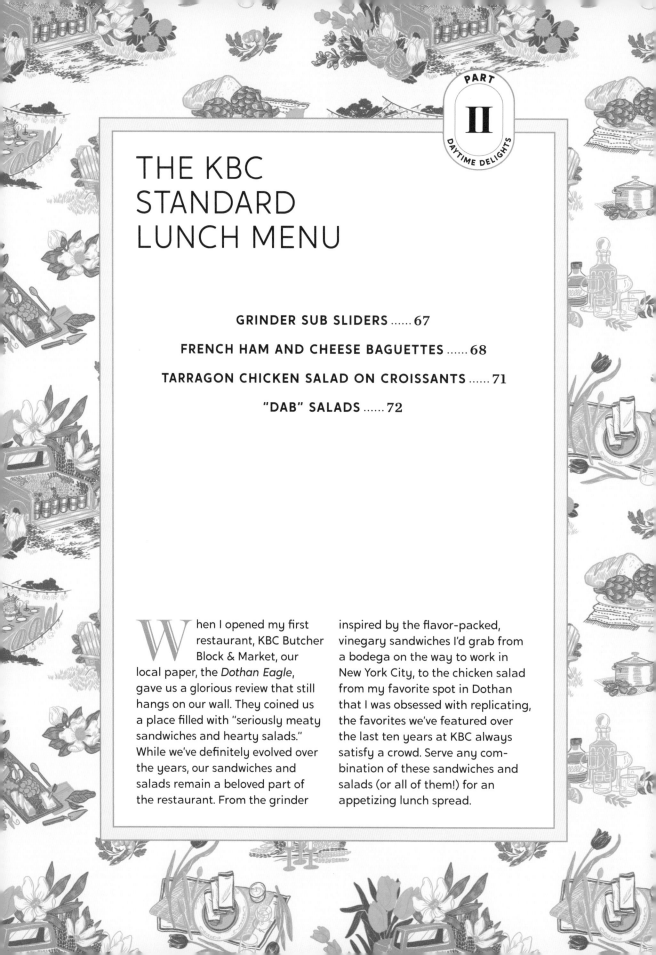

THE KBC STANDARD LUNCH MENU

When I opened my first restaurant, KBC Butcher Block & Market, our local paper, the *Dothan Eagle*, gave us a glorious review that still hangs on our wall. They coined us a place filled with "seriously meaty sandwiches and hearty salads." While we've definitely evolved over the years, our sandwiches and salads remain a beloved part of the restaurant. From the grinder inspired by the flavor-packed, vinegary sandwiches I'd grab from a bodega on the way to work in New York City, to the chicken salad from my favorite spot in Dothan that I was obsessed with replicating, the favorites we've featured over the last ten years at KBC always satisfy a crowd. Serve any combination of these sandwiches and salads (or all of them!) for an appetizing lunch spread.

Grinder Sub Sliders

SERVES 4 TO 6

½ head iceberg lettuce, shredded

1 small red onion, halved and thinly sliced

½ cup [50 g] drained and sliced pickled banana peppers

½ cup [70 g] pitted and sliced green olives

½ cup [150 g] drained and sliced pimiento peppers

1 cup [240 g] mayonnaise

2 Tbsp red wine vinegar

2 tsp dried Italian seasoning

Kosher salt

Freshly ground black pepper

8 oz [230 g] sliced provolone cheese, preferably square slices

1 baguette, halved lengthwise and toasted

4 oz [115 g] thinly sliced ham

4 oz [115 g] thinly sliced salami

4 oz [115 g] thinly sliced mortadella

2 tomatoes, cut into ¼ in [6 mm] thick slices

In a medium bowl, toss together the lettuce, red onion, banana peppers, olives, and pimiento peppers. Add the mayonnaise, vinegar, and Italian seasoning. Season with salt and pepper and toss to coat the salad mixture.

Cut each square slice of provolone diagonally in half to create two triangles (or two half-moons if the slices are round). Layer the bottom of the baguette with the provolone, ham, salami, mortadella, and tomatoes, then top with the salad mixture. Place the top of the baguette on the sandwich and use a bread knife to cut it crosswise into 2 to 3 in [5 to 7.5 cm] slices. Use short skewers or toothpicks to secure the slices for serving. Enjoy immediately.

French Ham and Cheese Baguettes

SERVES 4 TO 6

4 Tbsp [55 g] unsalted butter, at room temperature

1 baguette, halved lengthwise and toasted

3 Tbsp whole-grain mustard (I use Maille)

8 oz [230 g] thinly sliced unsmoked ham

8 oz [230 g] thinly sliced Gruyère, Brie, or Jarlsberg cheese

Spread the butter on one half of the baguette and spread the mustard on the other half. Layer the bottom of the baguette with the ham and cheese. Place the top of the baguette on the sandwich and use a bread knife to cut it crosswise into 2 to 3 in [5 to 7.5 cm] slices. Wrap each slice with parchment paper and tie with twine or use short skewers or toothpicks to secure them. Serve immediately.

> **NOTE**
> Because of the simplicity of this recipe, I recommend splurging on the highest-quality meat and cheese you can afford.

Tarragon Chicken Salad on Croissants

SERVES 4 TO 6

4 Tbsp [60 ml] tarragon vinegar

½ cup [70 g] golden raisins

3 lbs [1.4 kg] boiled and shredded chicken breasts

1 cup [240 g] mayonnaise

¼ cup [13 g] chopped fresh tarragon

2 Tbsp chopped fresh dill

1 Tbsp Dijon mustard

Kosher salt

Freshly ground black pepper

6 croissants, halved lengthwise

In a small pot, combine 2 Tbsp of the vinegar, the raisins, and enough water to just cover the raisins. Bring to a boil, then remove from the heat and set aside to rehydrate the raisins.

Meanwhile, in a medium bowl, combine the chicken, mayonnaise, tarragon, dill, mustard, and the remaining 2 Tbsp of vinegar and stir until completely combined.

Drain the raisins, then add them to the chicken mixture and stir to incorporate. Season with salt and pepper, then spoon onto the croissant bottoms, add the tops, and serve.

"Dab" Salads

(A DAB OF THIS, A DAB OF THAT!)

Tzatziki Fusilli Salad

SERVES 4 TO 6

4 cups [945 ml] chicken broth

Kosher salt

4 cups [372 g] fusilli pasta

1 cup [150 g] finely grated English cucumber

1 English cucumber, thinly sliced

One 6 oz [170 g] jar marinated artichoke hearts, drained and chopped

¼ cup [30 g] slivered dry-packed sun-dried tomatoes

1 cup [240 g] Greek yogurt

Zest and juice of 1 lemon

2 garlic cloves, grated

2 Tbsp chopped fresh dill

2 Tbsp chopped fresh flat-leaf parsley

1 Tbsp olive oil

Freshly ground black pepper

In a medium pot, bring the broth and 4 cups [945 ml] of water to a boil. Add 1 Tbsp of salt and the fusilli and cook, according to the package instructions, until al dente. Drain the fusilli, then put it in a medium bowl and add the grated cucumber, sliced cucumber, artichoke hearts, sun-dried tomatoes, yogurt, lemon zest and juice, garlic, dill, parsley, and olive oil. Toss to coat the pasta and vegetables, then season with salt and pepper. Serve immediately or refrigerate in an airtight container for up to 3 days.

French Onion Broccoli Salad

SERVES 4 TO 6

1 head broccoli

½ cup [85 g] slivered red or green grapes

1 bunch green onions, green and white parts, chopped

2 Tbsp chopped fresh dill

½ cup [130 g] Dean's or Lay's French onion dip (this is not a joke)

3 Tbsp olive oil

2 Tbsp rice wine vinegar

Zest and juice of 1 lemon

1 Tbsp everything bagel seasoning

1 cup [50 g] crushed potato chips

Cut off the florets from the head of broccoli, then peel and chop the stems. In a medium bowl, toss the broccoli florets and stems with the grapes, green onions, and dill. Add the French onion dip, olive oil, vinegar, lemon zest and juice, and everything bagel seasoning and toss to coat. Garnish with the crushed potato chips and serve immediately or refrigerate in an airtight container for up to 3 days, garnishing when ready to serve. cont.

Lemon–Poppy Seed Couscous and Cabbage Salad

SERVES 4 TO 6

2 cups [280 g] Israeli (pearl) couscous

3 cups [710 ml] chicken stock

1 cup [240 ml] olive oil, plus 1 Tbsp for cooking

4 cups [240 g] freshly shredded green cabbage

2 cups [200 g] chopped cauliflower

1 cup [140 g] chopped toasted hazelnuts or walnuts

1 bunch green onions, green and white parts, finely chopped

3 garlic cloves, minced

¼ cup [10 g] chopped fresh flat-leaf parsley

1 Tbsp chopped fresh dill

1 Tbsp chiffonade fresh basil

¼ cup [60 g] Greek yogurt or sour cream

Zest and juice of 2 lemons

2 Tbsp balsamic vinegar

1 Tbsp honey

2 Tbsp poppy seeds

1 Tbsp dried oregano

1 Tbsp dried thyme

1 Tbsp kosher salt

10 to 12 turns freshly ground black pepper

In a medium saucepan, bring the couscous, stock, and the 1 Tbsp of olive oil to a boil over high heat. Cover, lower the heat to a simmer, and cook until the couscous is soft and the liquid is absorbed, about 10 minutes. Uncover and let cool.

Meanwhile, in a medium bowl, combine the remaining 1 cup [240 ml] olive oil, cabbage, cauliflower, hazelnuts, green onions, garlic,

parsley, dill, basil, yogurt, lemon zest and juice, vinegar, and honey. Sprinkle with the poppy seeds, oregano, thyme, salt, and pepper. Toss until fully combined. Taste and season with more salt and pepper as necessary. Once the couscous has cooled, toss with the salad mixture. Let stand at room temperature for 30 minutes before serving or refrigerate in an airtight container for up to 3 days.

Arugula and Parmesan Salad

SERVES 4 TO 6

8 cups [160 g] baby arugula

½ cup [35 g] shaved Parmesan cheese

Zest and juice of 1 lemon

½ cup [120 ml] olive oil

Kosher salt

Freshly ground black pepper

In a medium bowl, toss together the arugula, Parmesan, lemon zest and juice, and olive oil. Season with salt and pepper and serve promptly to avoid the arugula wilting.

HAPPY HOURS AND STOP BYS

I love a happy hour, y'all. And while planned gatherings are lovely, I've come to embrace the impromptu. I'm in a season of life where my job and travel schedule are irregular. Throw in two kids and my husband's work travels, and if I want to enjoy a drink and snack with friends, I have to seize the moment when one presents itself. For me, a "Want to come over right now?" text is where it's at.

Happy hours are full of our favorite things. We all loved snacks as kids, and we love them just the same (maybe more?) as adults. Hello nostalgia. And while snacking boards may be having a moment, they're also an entertaining classic. When done well, they are beautiful, functional, and easy as heck for a host—especially with the recipes I've provided that ensure you cover all your bases!

Spontaneous get-togethers make me think of Mrs. Susan, the mom of one of my best friends. Mrs. Susan always had a bowl of her famous homemade Chex mix ready for our gaggle of teenage girls. While she busied herself in the kitchen, we'd sit there satisfying our appetites and gossiping about all the things. Her home always felt so warm and welcoming, and I'm pretty sure she knew more about our lives than any other mom because of those delicious bowls of Chex mix. My version of her recipe is a perfect addition to a grazing board.

When you're prepared for a spur-of-the-moment gathering, you get to focus on your guests. The recipes in this section build on the Party-Ready Pantry (see page 18) and Party-Ready Bar (see page 20) and are designed to put that preparation into action.

Flatbread Board

SERVES 4 TO 6

1 lb [455 g] frozen pizza dough

Toppings (recipes follow)

Prosciutto and Goat Cheese–Stuffed Dates (recipe follows)

Preheat the oven to 500°F [260°C].

Thaw frozen pizza dough for about 30 minutes or microwave it for a few minutes until it is pliable enough to roll out. On a floured work surface, roll out the dough to your desired thickness (I prefer ¼ inch [6 mm] thick for flatbreads), then place it on a lightly floured baking sheet. Add toppings for the flatbread version you desire (variations follow).

Arrange the flatbread squares and stuffed dates on a wooden board, or, if serving several types of flatbread, arrange each type on its own board and display the boards together.   cont.

II

Classic Flatbread

One 24 oz [680 g] jar tomato sauce

8 oz [230 g] fresh sliced mozzarella

Fresh basil, for garnish (optional)

Pesto, for garnish (optional)

Spread the tomato sauce on the dough, then arrange the sliced mozzarella on top. Bake the flatbread for about 15 minutes or until the cheese is bubbling and the crust is golden. Garnish with either fresh basil or a drizzle of pesto, cut into squares, and serve immediately.

Veggie and Olive Flatbread

1 cup [227 g] olive tapenade or olive salad

One 14½ oz [410 g] can whole stewed or diced fire-roasted tomatoes, drained

One 12 oz [340 g] jar marinated artichokes, drained

One 12 oz [340 g] jar marinated mushrooms, drained

8 oz [230 g] fresh sliced mozzarella

Pesto, for garnish (optional)

Balsamic vinegar, for garnish (optional)

Chili crunch, for garnish (optional)

Spread the olive tapenade or olive salad on the dough. Arrange the tomatoes, artichokes, and mushrooms on top, followed by the mozzarella. Bake the flatbread for about 15 minutes or until the cheese is bubbling and the crust is golden. Garnish with a drizzle of pesto and/or balsamic vinegar, or with a drizzle of chili crunch if you like a little spice. Cut into squares and serve immediately.

Garlic and Parmesan Flatbread

2 cups [60 g] grated Parmesan cheese

One 4½ oz [130 g] jar minced garlic

¼ cup [60 ml] olive oil

¼ cup [40 g] everything bagel seasoning

In a medium bowl, combine the Parmesan, garlic, and olive oil. Spread the Parmesan mixture on the dough. Bake the flatbread for about 15 minutes or until the cheese is bubbling and the crust is golden. Sprinkle with the everything bagel seasoning, cut into squares, and serve immediately.

Prosciutto and Goat Cheese– Stuffed Dates

SERVES 6 TO 8

14 to 16 Medjool dates, pitted

4 oz [115 g] goat cheese

7 to 8 prosciutto slices, halved lengthwise

Balsamic vinegar or balsamic glaze, for drizzling

Using a small spoon, gently stuff the dates with the goat cheese, closing the dates around the filling. Wrap a slice of prosciutto around each date and secure with a small skewer or toothpick. Drizzle with balsamic vinegar or glaze and serve.

Grazing Board

SERVES 4 TO 6

Cajun Pickled Okra Pimiento Cheese (recipe follows)

One 14 oz [400 g] jar olive tapenade or bruschetta topping

One 10 oz [285 g] container hummus

Crostini (recipe follows)

One 7 oz [200 g] bag pita chips

½ recipe Mrs. Susan's Animal House Chex Mix (recipe follows)

One 2½ to 3 oz [70 to 85 g] bag microwave popcorn, prepared according to the package instructions

To arrange snacks, start by putting the pimiento cheese, olive tapenade or bruschetta topping, and hummus in small bowls. Place the bowls on the perimeter of a flat platter (I like to use wood), then combine like with like—crostini nestled next to the tapenade or bruschetta topping, pita chips next to the hummus and pimiento cheese. Lastly, fill larger bowls with the Chex mix and popcorn and place them near the platter or on it if it's large enough. Provide small forks and spoons for serving.

Cajun Pickled Okra Pimiento Cheese

SERVES 4 TO 6

1 cup [80 g] freshly grated extra-sharp Cheddar cheese

⅓ cup [25 g] freshly grated smoked Gouda

½ cup [150 g] chopped pimiento peppers, drained

6 pickled okra, drained and chopped

¼ cup [60 g] sour cream

¼ cup [60 g] mayonnaise

1 tsp Old Bay Seasoning

¼ tsp smoked paprika

Kosher salt

Freshly ground black pepper

In a medium bowl, combine the Cheddar, Gouda, pimientos, okra, sour cream, mayonnaise, Old Bay, and smoked paprika and stir with a wooden spoon until completely combined. Season with salt and pepper. Serve chilled or at room temperature—try it with pork rinds! The vinegar from the pickled okra makes the dip last longer—keep it refrigerated in an airtight container for up to 1 week.

Crostini

MAKES 20 TO 25 PIECES

1 loaf French bread, cut crosswise into ½ in [12 mm] slices

3 Tbsp olive oil

1 Tbsp kosher salt

Preheat the oven to 350°F [175°C]. Line a baking sheet with parchment paper.

Place the bread slices in a single layer on the prepared baking sheet. Drizzle with the olive oil, sprinkle with the salt, and bake for 15 to 20 minutes, or until golden and crispy. Serve immediately or store in an airtight container for up to 1 month.   cont.

> **NOTE**
> I always use freshly grated cheese. Pre-shredded cheese is coated with cellulose to prevent clumping, which can be helpful, but the cheese lacks the flavor and creaminess of freshly grated. It also fails to melt properly and tends to dry out faster.

Mrs. Susan's Animal House Chex Mix

SERVES 10 TO 15

4 cups [905 g] unsalted butter

6 Tbsp [90 ml] Worcestershire sauce

8 to 10 dashes Tabasco or Crystal hot sauce

1 Tbsp garlic powder

1 Tbsp onion powder

3 to 4 Tbsp seasoned salt, such as Lawry's

4 cups [600 g] mixed unsalted nuts

One 1 lb [455 g] bag pretzel snaps

One 14 oz [400 g] bag Gardetto's garlic rye chips

One 14 oz [400 g] box wheat Chex cereal

One 12 oz [340 g] box rice Chex cereal

One 12 oz [340 g] box corn Chex cereal

One 12 oz [340 g] box Original Cheerios cereal

One 12 oz [340 g] box Cheez-It crackers

One 6⅔ oz [185 g] bag Goldfish crackers

Preheat the oven to 250°F [120°C]. Line four to six large baking sheets with parchment paper, or do this in batches using two baking sheets. In a medium saucepan, melt the butter over medium heat. Remove from the heat and whisk in the Worcestershire sauce, hot sauce, garlic powder, onion powder, and seasoned salt.

In a very large bowl or multiple smaller vessels, toss together the nuts, pretzels, rye chips, cereals, and crackers. Add the butter mixture and toss to coat. Taste and add more seasoned salt as needed. Spread the mixture in a single layer on the prepared baking sheets and bake, stirring every 15 minutes, for 45 minutes to 1 hour, or until lightly browned and crispy. Let cool completely before serving or store in airtight containers for up to 1 week, or freeze in sealed bags for up to 3 months. When ready to use, thaw the Chex mix at room temperature or reheat it in a 300°F [150°C] oven for about 10 minutes.

Charcuterie Board

SERVES 6 TO 8

Two 4 oz [115 g] wedges hard cheese (see Note)

Two 4 oz [115 g] wedges or small rounds soft cheese (see Note)

Two 4 oz [115 g] wedges or small rounds semisoft cheese (see Note)

12 to 16 oz [340 to 455 g] mixed olives or Warm Marinated Olives (recipe follows)

8 to 12 oz [230 to 340 g] cured meats, such as prosciutto, salami, soppressata, bresaola, capicola, or coppa

8 to 10 oz [230 to 285 g] jelly or jam of your choice (fig jam and pepper jelly are my go-tos)

6 to 10 Tbsp [120 to 200 g] honey or truffle honey or one 3 in [7.5 cm] square of honeycomb

1 bunch red or green grapes

10 to 12 oz [285 to 340 g] mixed unsalted nuts

6 to 8 oz [170 to 230 g] dried fruit, such as jumbo raisins, apricots, dates, or figs

12 oz to 1¼ lb [340 to 570 g] artisan crackers (use three varieties of crackers, flatbreads, bagel chips, crostini, or pita bread)

On a large flat platter or wooden board, arrange the cheeses spaced out from one another. Next, place the olives in a medium bowl and set the bowl in the middle of the platter. Separate the cured meats and arrange them, fanned out (do not serve them in a ball!), next to the cheeses. Place the jars of jelly or jam and honey on opposite sides of the board. Next, pull small bunches from the grapes and use those, along with handfuls of nuts, dried fruits, and crackers, to fill in the empty spaces. Cut a few slices of each of the hard cheeses and a little wedge of each of the soft and semisoft cheeses ahead of time to encourage guests to dig in. Be sure there are enough knives and spoons so that each item has its own.

Warm Marinated Olives

SERVES 4 TO 6

24 oz [680 g] mixed olives, such as
Castelvetrano, Greek, Kalamata, and
Manzanillo

½ cup [45 g] jarred mild, whole peppadew
peppers

1 small lemon, cut into ¼ in [6 mm]
thick rounds

1 small orange, cut into ¼ in [6 mm]
thick rounds

2 garlic cloves

¼ cup [60 ml] olive oil

1 Tbsp balsamic vinegar

1 bay leaf

½ tsp dried thyme

½ tsp dried rosemary

½ tsp fennel seeds

In a small pot, combine the olives, peppers,
lemon, orange, garlic, olive oil, vinegar, bay
leaf, thyme, rosemary, and fennel seeds,
and bring to a simmer over medium heat.
Continue simmering for 15 minutes, then
remove from the heat and let stand at room
temperature for about 20 minutes before
serving. Serve immediately or refrigerate
in an airtight container for up to 1 month. If
refrigerated, let the olives sit out at room
temperature for 20 to 30 minutes before
serving.

> **NOTE**
>
> **HARD CHEESES INCLUDE:**
> aged Cheddar, aged Gouda,
> Comté, Grana Padano,
> Gruyère.
>
> **SOFT CHEESES INCLUDE:**
> Boursin, Brie, Camembert,
> goat, Époisses, Fromager
> d'Affinois, Humboldt
> Fog, Jarlsberg, Muenster,
> Taleggio, triple-crème.
>
> **SEMISOFT CHEESES INCLUDE:**
> fontina, Havarti, Limburger,
> pepper jack, Reblochon,
> Roquefort, smoked Gouda,
> Stilton.

Classic Cocktails

Sazerac

MAKES 1 DRINK

2 oz [60 ml] bourbon
5 drops bitters
Lemon twist, for garnish

Add the bourbon and bitters to an ice-filled mixing glass. Stir until well chilled, about 30 seconds. Strain into a rocks glass and garnish with the lemon twist.

Mint Julep

MAKES 1 DRINK

2 oz [60 ml] bourbon
2 fresh mint sprigs
3 oz [90 ml] simple syrup
2 to 3 oz [60 to 90 ml] soda water

Add the bourbon and 1 sprig of fresh mint to a rocks glass or julep cup and briefly muddle. Add the simple syrup and stir to combine. Fill the glass with ice, add a splash of soda water, and garnish with a sprig of fresh mint.

Moscow Mule

MAKES 1 DRINK

2 oz [60 ml] vodka
1 oz [30 ml] fresh lime juice
4 to 6 oz [120 to 180 ml] ginger beer
Lime wedge, for garnish

Add the vodka and lime juice to an ice-filled copper mug, julep cup, or rocks glass. Finish with the ginger beer, stir, and garnish with the lime wedge.

MEXICAN MULE
Swap the vodka for tequila to make a Mexican mule—my favorite!

Old Fashioned

MAKES 1 DRINK

1 sugar cube
2 dashes bitters
2 oz [60 ml] bourbon
1 large ice cube
Orange twist, for garnish

Add the sugar cube and bitters to a rocks glass and muddle until the sugar dissolves. Add the bourbon, stir, and add a large cube of ice. Wipe the orange twist around the rim, then drop it into the glass.

PART

III

SOUTHERN GET-TOGETHERS

All-Day Bashes

All-day bashes—gatherings with a start time but no end time and which often take on a life of their own—are a social indulgence. A day spent fishing that ends with a low country boil, some great storytelling, and maybe a little karaoke, or a shared nightcap at the bar down the street after the playoff game. In our fast-paced, highly scheduled lives, it's not always easy to carve out time to just hang out, be present, and let the day unfold.

I especially love hosting all-day affairs al fresco, where sunlight sets the pace of the day, and the unexpected adds a little thrill, whether a sudden rainstorm or a mesmerizing full moon lighting up the sky. When I lived in the city, I was all about packing it up and heading to a park; hanging out on the stoop, the rooftop, or the fire escape after a meal; or even just opening the windows and bringing plenty of green in. Now, my favorite places to host outside are my backyard at home in Alabama and our beach cottage in Florida. Wherever you are, I urge you to find your own way of inviting the magic of nature to be a special guest at your fete.

LOW COUNTRY BOIL

This Southern tradition of gathering around a newspaper-lined table and eating more than your share of fresh, spicy seafood with your bare hands is just so fun. Nothing about it is subtle, and everything about it is delicious. Of course, boils are my favorite meal to serve at the beach. There's nothing like coming in after a day spent on the water, in the heat of the sun, skin tasting of salt, and getting a boil going while we refresh ourselves with a cocktail. The success of a boil depends on the layering, the timing, the salt, and the spice. If you are sneezing while spicing, and your nose is running when you taste your broth, then you've got a good one, y'all.

Low Country Boil

SERVES 10 TO 15

One 3 oz [85 g] package seafood boil seasoning

One 8 oz [230 g] jar Better Than Bouillon fish base

2½ lbs [1.1 kg] button mushrooms, trimmed

2 lbs [910 g] smoky, spicy sausage, cut into bite-size pieces

5 to 8 whole artichokes, halved vertically

5 to 8 ears fresh corn, shucked and halved

5 jalapeños

2 large onions, chopped

1 head garlic

2 lbs [910 g] new potatoes

5 lbs [2.3 kg] shrimp, crab, head-on crawfish, or a combination

Old Bay Seasoning, for serving

1 bunch fresh flat-leaf parsley, leaves chopped

1 bunch fresh cilantro, leaves chopped

2 lemons, halved

2 cups [450 g] unsalted butter, melted

Tabasco or Crystal hot sauce, for serving

Cover a serving table with newspaper or butcher paper. Set out seafood crackers or small wooden hammers to crack the seafood, as well as bowls for discarding any shells.

Fill a low country boil pot (a large, deep pot with a fitted colander basket) with the seafood boil seasoning, fish base, mushrooms, sausage, artichokes, corn, jalapeños, onions, and garlic. Add enough water to fill the pot three-quarters of the way and bring to a rolling boil. Continue boiling for at least 30 minutes or up to 1 hour. Add the potatoes and boil for 20 minutes. Add the seafood and boil for 20 minutes if using crab or crawfish, or 10 to 15 minutes if using shrimp, or until the shrimp turn pink. Lift the colander basket out of the pot, draining the boil, then pour it out onto the paper-lined table. Sprinkle with the Old Bay, parsley, and cilantro and squeeze the lemons over the top. Serve with melted butter and hot sauce on the side.

OYSTER ROAST
AND CHILI DOGS

PART

III

ALL-DAY BASHES

While it may seem like an odd combination, you will be hard pressed to find an oyster bar in the South that doesn't also serve chili dogs. And it's genius—those who don't love these gems on the half shell can enjoy the all-American, ever-so-satisfying hot dog. And let's be real: Oysters do not fill you up. This menu is a perfect fit for a laid-back, all-afternoon gathering like a game day. Oysters make an obvious starter, and when guests' hunger returns later, they can tuck into the dogs and chili bar. Just be sure to watch the oysters closely—you don't want to overcook these wonderful, tender mollusks!

Garlic Butter–Mopped Oysters

SERVES 4 TO 6

Garlic Butter Mop

2 cups [450 g] unsalted butter, melted

6 garlic cloves, minced

2 Tbsp finely chopped fresh flat-leaf parsley

2 Tbsp finely chopped fresh chives

1 tsp Old Bay Seasoning

Pinch of cayenne pepper

Oysters

4 dozen raw oysters, shucked and left on the half shell (see facing page)

2 cups [120 g] grated pecorino romano cheese

1 lemon, halved, plus 2 lemons, cut into wedges

Crusty bread, sliced, for serving

Preheat the grill to 400°F [200°C].

To make the garlic butter mop: In a medium bowl, whisk together the melted butter, garlic, parsley, chives, Old Bay, and cayenne.

To make the oysters: Place the oysters on the half shell on the hottest part of the grill and let them cook in their own juices for 2 to 3 minutes, or until their edges just start to curl. Using a pastry brush or small barbecue mop, brush the oysters with enough garlic butter sauce to fill each shell—you should use all of the sauce. A little fire leaping up from any spilled sauce is normal. When the sauce starts to bubble, sprinkle each oyster with some pecorino romano and continue cooking until the sauce has browned around the edges. Remove the oysters from the grill, then squeeze the halved lemon over the top. Serve immediately, with the lemon wedges and a basket of sliced, crusty bread for sopping up the leftover sauce.

HOW TO SHUCK OYSTERS
LIKE A PRO:

1

On a sturdy work surface, fold a kitchen towel into a square (no, we don't use gloves) and place an oyster on top of the towel with the flat side of the shell facing up.

2

Fold the towel halfway over the oyster, with the knuckle side facing out. Hold the oyster down firmly with the palm of your nondominant hand.

3

Holding the oyster knife in your dominant hand, position the flat side of the blade parallel to the shell, then wiggle and press the tip of the knife into the hinge until you feel a soft spot.

4

Press the knife in, then twist it back and forth and wiggle it until the shell pops open. Scrape your knife under the oyster and along the shell to cut the adductor muscle and completely free the oyster.

Oysters Rockefeller

SERVES 4 TO 6

½ cup [113 g] unsalted butter

4 cups [560 g] minced onion or shallot

4 celery stalks, minced

4 garlic cloves, minced

4 cups [80 g] packed baby spinach leaves, stemmed

¼ cup [60 ml] Pernod

Kosher salt

Freshly ground black pepper

2 dashes Tabasco or Crystal hot sauce

1 cup [60 g] panko

1 cup [30 g] grated Parmesan cheese

½ cup [20 g] finely chopped fresh flat-leaf parsley

4 dozen oysters, shucked and left on the half shell

Lemon wedges, for serving

Saltine crackers, for serving

Preheat the grill to 400°F [200°C].

In a medium skillet or sauté pan, melt the butter over medium heat. Add the onion or shallot, celery, and garlic and sauté until translucent, 3 to 5 minutes. Add the spinach and sauté until the spinach wilts, about 2 minutes. Add the Pernod and deglaze the pan, stirring to scrape up the browned bits from the bottom. Continue cooking until the liquid has all but evaporated. Season with salt and pepper, then add the hot sauce. Remove from the heat.

In a small bowl, combine the panko, Parmesan, and parsley.

Evenly distribute the spinach mixture, followed by the panko mixture, on top of the oysters on the half shell. Place the topped oysters on the hottest part of the grill and cook for 3 to 5 minutes, or until the topping is bubbling and golden. Serve with lemon wedges and saltine crackers.

Hot Dog Chili and the Fixins

SERVES 8

Hot Dog Chili

2 Tbsp olive oil

1 lb [455 g] lean ground beef (80/20)

1 onion, chopped

4 garlic cloves, minced

1 jalapeño, minced

2 cups [475 ml] beef broth

½ cup [120 ml] tomato sauce

2 Tbsp tomato paste

2 Tbsp chili powder

1 Tbsp Worcestershire sauce

1 Tbsp soy sauce

1 Tbsp Tabasco or Crystal hot sauce

1 Tbsp paprika

1 tsp ground cumin

Pinch of cayenne pepper

8 to 10 turns freshly ground black pepper

Kosher salt

Hot Dogs

8 hot dogs

8 hot dog buns

Fixins (see My Favorite Fixins)

MY FAVORITE FIXINS

- Chopped onions
- Corn chips
- Corn nuts
- Fried garlic
- Fried onions
- Green onions
- Ketchup
- Mustard
- Pickled jalapeños
- Pickled okra
- Pickles
- Shredded Cheddar cheese
- Sour cream

To make the hot dog chili: In a large skillet, heat the olive oil over medium-high heat. Add the ground beef and cook, stirring and breaking up the meat, for about 10 minutes, or until slightly browned. Using a slotted spoon, transfer the meat to a medium bowl. Add the onion, garlic, and jalapeño to the skillet and sauté, stirring, for 5 minutes, or until the onion is caramelized. Add the beef broth, tomato sauce, tomato paste, chili powder, Worcestershire sauce, soy sauce, hot sauce, paprika, cumin, cayenne, and black pepper and bring to a boil. Lower the heat to a simmer and cook, stirring, until the chili is thick and the liquid has reduced almost completely. Season with salt. Enjoy immediately or refrigerate in an airtight container for up to 3 days.

To make the hot dogs: Cook the hot dogs as you wish—on the grill, in boiling water, or in the microwave—then place in a bun and top with chili, if desired, and fixins.

GAME DAY

When we say "Game Day" in the South, we're either talking about high school Friday night football, which we watch in person, or we're talking about Saturday SEC college football, which typically means an all-day, kids-and-adults gathering at someone's house to watch the game on TV. During this highly anticipated season, die-hard fans have to temporarily abandon friend groups or couples who root for the rival team to avoid what could become an inappropriate and unforgivable encounter. All joking aside, when I host game day, I keep in mind that the food needs to be casual—mostly finger food, ideally—and must be able to sit out to allow for grazing throughout the afternoon. If I'm pinched for time (or energy), sometimes I prepare only the meat and ask guests to bring apps and sides— potato salad, pasta salad, slaw, mac & cheese, roasted potatoes, baked beans, or any type of green salad all work well with my brisket. And if you aren't a football fan, this menu works well for any daylong gathering—think backyard barbecues, family reunions, or the Fourth of July.

KBC's Smoked Brisket

SERVES 10 TO 12

Barbecue Dry Rub

2 cups [400 g] light brown sugar

1 cup [240 g] coarse kosher salt

½ cup [55 g] paprika

¼ cup [28 g] onion powder

¼ cup [28 g] garlic powder

3 Tbsp ground ginger

Barbecue Sauce

4 cups [880 g] ketchup

1 cup [240 ml] apple cider vinegar

6 Tbsp [90 g] light brown sugar

3 Tbsp yellow mustard

3 Tbsp Worcestershire sauce

1 Tbsp freshly ground black pepper

1 Tbsp red pepper flakes

Barbecue Brisket

About 4 cups [280 g] maple, hickory, or oak wood chips (or enough to cover the bottom of the grill)

One 8 to 11 lb [3.6 to 5 kg] brisket

To make the barbecue dry rub: In a small bowl, combine the brown sugar, salt, paprika, onion powder, garlic powder, and ginger. Set aside. The rub can be made in bulk and stored in an airtight container in your pantry for up to 3 months.

To make the barbecue sauce: In a small saucepan, whisk together the ketchup, vinegar, brown sugar, mustard, Worcestershire sauce, black pepper, and red pepper flakes. Bring to a simmer and continue simmering for 15 to 20 minutes, or until the sugar is dissolved. Continue cooking the sauce for up to 30 minutes for optimum flavor. Remove from the heat. The sauce can be made in bulk and stored in an airtight container in the refrigerator for up to 3 months.

To cook the brisket: First, prepare the wood chips. In a clean bucket or large bowl, cover the wood chips with water and soak for at least 1 hour.

While the wood chips are soaking, prepare the brisket. Pat the brisket with paper towels until completely dry, then cover thoroughly with the dry rub.

If smoking the brisket on a grill: Heat a gas or charcoal grill until hot, 225°F to 250°F [107°C to 120°C], then add the wood chips. Heat until the grill begins to smoke, then add the brisket and maintain low heat for 1 to 2 hours. Next, follow the braising instructions below.

If smoking the brisket without a grill: Add the wood chips to the bottom of a large pot with a basket insert. The basket of the pot needs to be large enough to fit the brisket either whole or cut in half. Insert the basket into the pot, then add the brisket to the basket and place it on the stove over medium heat. When you start to see smoke, cover the pot with a lid, then wrap it very tightly with aluminum foil so that no smoke can escape. Turn the heat to low and smoke the brisket for 30 minutes to 1 hour. Next, follow the braising instructions below.

After smoking on the grill or on the stovetop, braise the brisket: Preheat the oven to 250°F [120°C]. Place the brisket and 3 cups [710 ml] of water in a roasting or braising pan, then cover the pan tightly with aluminum foil. Put the brisket in the oven and braise for 12 to 14 hours or overnight. The brisket is done when the meat easily pulls apart. Cool before cutting into slices or shredding. Serve with the barbecue sauce for dipping.

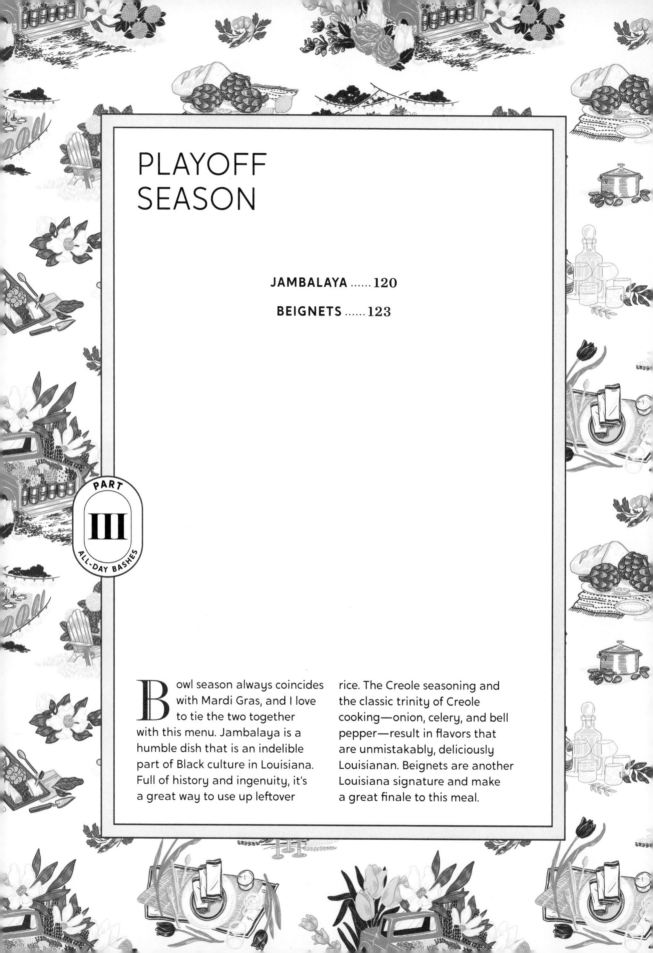

PLAYOFF SEASON

PART

III

ALL-DAY BASHES

Bowl season always coincides with Mardi Gras, and I love to tie the two together with this menu. Jambalaya is a humble dish that is an indelible part of Black culture in Louisiana. Full of history and ingenuity, it's a great way to use up leftover rice. The Creole seasoning and the classic trinity of Creole cooking—onion, celery, and bell pepper—result in flavors that are unmistakably, deliciously Louisianan. Beignets are another Louisiana signature and make a great finale to this meal.

Jambalaya

SERVES 4 TO 6

1 lb [455 g] andouille sausage or any spicy smoked sausage, cut into half-moons

2 Tbsp unsalted butter

2 Tbsp all-purpose flour

4 celery stalks, chopped

1 onion, chopped

1 bell pepper, chopped

2 jalapeños, chopped

4 garlic cloves, minced

5 cups [1.2 L] Shrimp Stock (recipe follows)

One 15 oz [425 g] can crushed tomatoes

1 cup [200 g] jasmine rice

2 Tbsp tomato paste

2 Tbsp Old Bay Seasoning, plus more as needed

1 Tbsp smoked paprika

1 Tbsp Tabasco or Crystal hot sauce, plus more as needed

2 fresh thyme sprigs

2 bay leaves

1 tsp dried oregano

Pinch of saffron threads

2 lbs [910 g] shell-on large or jumbo shrimp

1 tsp filé powder or 6 bay leaves

Kosher salt

½ cup [20 g] chopped fresh flat-leaf parsley

1 cup [100 g] chopped green onions, green and white parts

In a large Dutch oven over medium heat, cook the sausage for 10 minutes, or until the fat has rendered and the sausage is golden. Transfer the sausage to a paper towel–lined plate and set aside. Add the butter and flour to the Dutch oven and whisk them into the fat for 10 to 15 minutes, or until a milk chocolate–colored roux forms. Add the celery, onion, bell pepper, jalapeños, and garlic and cook, stirring, for 5 more minutes. Add the shrimp stock, crushed tomatoes, rice, tomato paste, Old Bay, smoked paprika, hot sauce, thyme, 2 bay leaves (or 8 bay leaves if you're using them in place of filé powder), oregano, and saffron and bring to a boil. Add the sausage, lower the heat to a simmer, cover, and cook for 15 minutes. Add the shrimp, stir to coat, and cook, covered, for 5 to 10 minutes, or until the rice is cooked through but not mushy. Stir in the filé powder, if using, and season with salt and more Old Bay as needed. Remove the thyme sprigs and bay leaves. Sprinkle with parsley, green onions, and hot sauce. Serve immediately. Store the cooled leftovers in an airtight container in the refrigerator for up to 3 days, or in the freezer for up to 6 months.

Shrimp Stock

MAKES ABOUT 4 CUPS [945 ML]

Shells from 2 lbs [910 g] shrimp

6 cups [1.4 L] chicken stock (or 6 cups water and ¼ cup [56 g] Better Than Bouillon roasted chicken base)

1 carrot, chopped

1 onion, chopped

1 celery stalk, chopped

1 Tbsp peppercorns

2 bay leaves

2 fresh thyme sprigs

In a large Dutch oven or stockpot over high heat, toast the shrimp shells for 2 minutes. Add the chicken stock, carrot, onion, celery, peppercorns, bay leaves, and thyme and bring to a boil. Turn the heat to a simmer and cook for 45 minutes. Strain the stock, then store in an airtight container in the refrigerator for up to 1 week or in the freezer for up to 3 months.

Beignets

SERVES 4 TO 6

¼ cup [50 g] granulated sugar

1½ tsp active dry yeast

3½ cups [490 g] all-purpose flour

½ cup [120 ml] whole or 2 percent milk, warm

5 Tbsp [75 g] unsalted butter, melted

1 large egg, beaten

1 tsp vanilla extract

⅛ tsp kosher salt, plus ½ tsp for dusting

6 cups [1.4 L] peanut or canola oil, for frying

1 cup [120 g] confectioners' sugar, for dusting

Paper bag

In the bowl of a stand mixer fitted with the dough hook attachment, stir together the granulated sugar, yeast, and ¾ cup [180 ml] of warm water. Let rest for 5 to 10 minutes, or until foamy.

Once the yeast mixture is foamy, add the flour, milk, butter, egg, vanilla, and the ⅛ tsp of salt. Mix on medium speed until the mixture is tacky and pulls around the dough hook. Remove the dough from the mixer, cover, and let rest in a warm area for up to 2 hours, or until it has doubled in size.

Once the dough has doubled in size, fill a deep fryer, rondeau, or wide, shallow pot with the peanut or canola oil and heat to 350°F [180°C].

Remove the dough from the bowl and lightly knead it on a floured work surface. Use a rolling pin to roll out the dough until about ¼ in [6 mm] thick. Using a pizza cutter, cut the beignets into 2 to 3 in [5 to 7.5 cm] squares. These do not need to be uniform; they are meant to be misshapen.

Working in batches, carefully drop the beignets in the hot oil and fry, flipping once, until lightly golden, about 2 minutes on each side. Repeat to fry the remaining beignets. Put the beignets in a paper bag with the remaining ½ tsp salt and the confectioners' sugar and shake to coat. Serve immediately.

CLASSIC FRY DAY FETE

PART

III

ALL-DAY BASHES

Fry day fetes are outside fry parties—my favorite place to fry to avoid the mess and smell. There is just something so celebratory and straight-up fun about a fry day fete. It just feels like a party, y'all. For most, it's rare to light up a fryer just any old day, and even more rare to do so for such a large gathering. You can either fry everything ahead of time and keep it all on baking sheets lined with racks or paper towels in a 300°F [150°C] oven until ready to serve, or fry as you go, dunking the basket after each devoured batch. This classic menu delivers comforting, nostalgic flavors. Hot Honey Chicken with Quick Pickled Green Tomatoes and a Zucchini Gratin is one of my favorite meals on the planet. Pair it with a cold glass of White Sparkling Sangria and cap it off with a big bowl of my mom's Shortbread Crumble Banana Pudding and you may as well call it my death row meal.

Hot Honey Chicken

SERVES 4 TO 6

OG Fried Chicken

4 cups [945 ml] buttermilk

1 cup [240 ml] dill pickle juice

6 to 8 dashes Tabasco or Crystal hot sauce

4 to 6 skin-on, bone-in chicken thighs, rinsed thoroughly and patted dry

5 cups [700 g] all-purpose flour

1 cup [140 g] cornstarch

2 Tbsp garlic powder

1 Tbsp onion powder

1 Tbsp kosher salt

1 Tbsp freshly ground black pepper

1 tsp cayenne pepper

4 to 8 cups [945 ml to 1.9 L] peanut or canola oil

Hot Honey Sauce

1 cup [340 g] honey

¼ cup [57 g] chili crunch

1 to 2 tsp cayenne pepper

1 tsp chili powder

1 tsp garlic powder

1 tsp paprika

To make the OG fried chicken: In a large bowl, stir together the buttermilk, pickle juice, and hot sauce. Add the chicken thighs to the buttermilk brine and refrigerate, covered, for at least 1 hour or up to 2 days. Let the chicken sit in the buttermilk brine at room temperature for 30 minutes before frying.

In a 9 by 13 in [23 by 33 cm] casserole dish, whisk together the flour, cornstarch, garlic powder, onion powder, salt, black pepper, and cayenne. One at a time, remove the chicken thighs from the buttermilk brine, shaking off any excess liquid, then dredge in the flour mixture, pressing the mixture onto the chicken until it is completely coated and feels dry to the touch. (See Note on page 130.) Place the coated chicken in a single layer on a plate.

Fill a deep fryer or a cast-iron skillet halfway with the peanut or canola oil and begin warming it over the lowest heat possible.
cont.

Meanwhile, make the hot honey sauce: In a large bowl, whisk together the honey, chili crunch, 1 tsp of cayenne, the chili powder, garlic powder, and paprika. Taste, then add more cayenne a pinch at a time to reach your desired spice level.

Turn the heat under the skillet to high and heat the oil to 400°F [200°C]. Set a rack inside a baking sheet and arrange it near the stovetop. Set the bowl of hot honey sauce next to the baking sheet. To test whether the oil is hot enough, drop a sprinkle of flour in the pan. If the flour pops and fizzes, the oil is ready.

Working in batches of two or three, carefully drop the chicken thighs in the hot oil. Immediately turn the heat to medium to allow the chicken to cook slowly and evenly while also developing a crispy golden crust. Using a long-handled fork, such as a carving fork, gently flip the chicken over every 2 minutes. Cook for 12 to 15 minutes, or until the chicken reaches an internal temperature of 165°F [74°C]. As soon as the chicken is done frying, use tongs to remove it from the oil and immediately dip it (still wet and dripping with oil) in the hot honey sauce, flipping the chicken to ensure it is fully coated, then place it on the rack set in the baking sheet and let cool for 5 to 10 minutes before eating. Cooling the chicken on a rack allows the excess oil to drip off while leaving the bottom of the chicken crispy. Repeat to fry and dip the remaining chicken, adjusting the heat as needed. Enjoy immediately or keep warm in a 250°F [120°C] oven until ready to serve.

> **NOTE**
>
> To keep your hands from becoming a science fair project, use one hand for touching the brined chicken and the other for dredging. This ensures that only one hand is caked with the glue-like brine and flour.

Zucchini Gratin

SERVES 4 TO 6

4 zucchini (about 2 lbs [910 g] total), thinly sliced

2 Tbsp kosher salt

¾ cup [165 g] unsalted butter

3 onions, thinly sliced

8 to 10 turns freshly ground black pepper

¼ tsp ground nutmeg

2 Tbsp mushroom powder

2 Tbsp all-purpose flour

1 cup [240 ml] cream of mushroom soup

2 cups [160 g] grated aged Gouda or Parmesan cheese

1 bunch green onions, green and white parts, chopped

1 bunch fresh flat-leaf parsley, leaves chopped

½ cup [25 g] chopped fresh tarragon

¼ cup [5 g] chiffonade fresh basil

1 cup [60 g] panko

1 cup [115 g] grated Gruyère cheese

Pinch of red pepper flakes

Preheat the oven to 400°F [200°C]. Butter an 8 by 10 in [20 by 25 cm] baking dish.

In a large bowl, toss the zucchini with the salt, then let stand for 30 minutes, or until the zucchini has started to release its liquid. Drain and set aside.

In a large skillet over medium heat, melt ½ cup [110 g] of the butter. Add the onions and cook for 20 minutes, or until golden brown. Add the drained zucchini and cook for 10 more minutes. Add the black pepper, nutmeg, and mushroom powder, then sprinkle with the flour. Add the cream of mushroom soup, turn the heat to a simmer, and cook for 3 to 5 minutes, or until the liquid thickens into a sauce. Stir in the Gouda or Parmesan, green onions, parsley, tarragon, and basil, then pour the mixture into the prepared baking dish.

In a small saucepan, melt the remaining 4 Tbsp [55 g] of butter. Add the panko, Gruyère, and red pepper flakes and stir to combine. Spoon the panko mixture over the zucchini mixture and bake for 20 minutes, or until bubbly and golden brown on top. Let cool for 10 to 15 minutes before serving. Enjoy warm or at room temperature or cover tightly in aluminum foil or plastic wrap and refrigerate for up to 3 days. Reheat in a 400°F [200°C] oven for 15 to 20 minutes.

NOTE

This dish is an easy one to make ahead. After spooning the panko mixture over the zucchini mixture, cover tightly with aluminum foil or plastic wrap and refrigerate for up to 3 days or freeze for up to 3 months. Thaw, if frozen, and let come to room temperature before baking.

Quick Pickled Green Tomatoes

SERVES 4 TO 6

3 cups [710 ml] apple cider vinegar

¼ cup [60 g] kosher salt

¼ cup [40 g] mustard seeds

¼ cup [40 g] coriander seeds

¼ cup [30 g] dill seeds

4 to 6 bay leaves

1 Tbsp granulated sugar

4 green tomatoes, cut into ½ in [13 mm] rounds, or 4 cups [600 g] green cherry tomatoes, halved

1 onion, thinly sliced

6 to 8 garlic cloves, peeled

In a medium pot, combine the vinegar, salt, mustard seeds, coriander seeds, dill seeds, bay leaves, sugar, and 3 cups [710 ml] of water and bring to a boil. Continue boiling until the sugar and salt are dissolved, then remove from the heat.

In a 9 by 13 in [23 by 33 cm] casserole dish, combine the tomatoes, onion, and garlic. Add the pickling liquid and let cool to room temperature. Enjoy right away or store in an airtight container in the refrigerator for up to 1 week.

NOTE

If you can't find green tomatoes, use the firmest red tomatoes you can find.

Shortbread Crumble Banana Pudding

SERVES 4 TO 6

Pudding

Two 3.4 oz [96 g] boxes instant vanilla pudding

1 tsp vanilla extract

Whipped Cream

2 cups [475 ml] heavy cream

½ cup [60 g] confectioners' sugar

1 tsp vanilla extract

Pinch of kosher salt

Shortbread Crumble

2 cups [452 g] unsalted butter, at room temperature

2 cups [400 g] granulated sugar

2 tsp kosher salt

3 large egg yolks

1 Tbsp vanilla extract

5 cups [700 g] all-purpose flour

5 ripe bananas

To make the pudding: Prepare the vanilla pudding following the directions on the box, then stir in the vanilla. Cover and refrigerate to cool.

To make the whipped cream: In the bowl of a stand mixer fitted with the whisk attachment, combine the heavy cream, confectioners' sugar, vanilla, and salt and whip on low speed for 2 minutes. Gradually increase the speed to high and whip for 1 to 2 minutes, or until stiff peaks form. Use immediately or refrigerate for a few hours or overnight.   **cont.**

To make the shortbread crumble: Preheat the oven to 325°F [165°C]. Line a baking sheet with parchment paper.

In the bowl of a stand mixer fitted with the paddle attachment, combine the butter, granulated sugar, and salt and beat on medium speed, scraping down the sides of the bowl as needed, for about 5 minutes, or until pale yellow and smooth. (Do not beat until fluffy; you don't want to incorporate air into the dough.) Add the egg yolks and vanilla and mix for about 1 minute, or until just combined. Turn the mixer off and scrape down the sides of the bowl. Add the flour and scrape down the bottom and sides of the bowl. Mix on low speed, scraping the bowl as needed, for about 1 minute, or until the flour is fully incorporated. The dough will be in large crumbles. Wrap and refrigerate for later use or spread the dough crumbles on the prepared baking sheet. Bake, turning the baking sheet every few minutes for even baking, for 20 to 30 minutes, or until light golden and slightly crunchy. Let cool before using.

To assemble: Peel and cut the bananas into ⅓ in [8.5 mm] thick slices. In a 9 by 13 in [23 by 33 cm] dish, layer the pudding, bananas, whipped cream, and shortbread crumble, repeating until all the ingredients are used up. Enjoy immediately or cover with aluminum foil or plastic wrap and refrigerate for up to 3 days.

White Sparkling Sangria

MAKES 1 PITCHER (4 TO 6 DRINKS)

One 750 ml bottle dry white wine, such as Pinot Grigio,
Sauvignon Blanc, or Chardonnay

1 cup [240 ml] grapefruit juice

1 grapefruit, halved and cut into ¼ in [6 mm] slices

1 orange, halved and cut into ¼ in [6 mm] slices

2 cups [240 g] strawberries, halved

1 cup [140 g] chopped pineapple

One 750 ml bottle Cava or prosecco

In a large pitcher, combine the white wine, grapefruit juice,
grapefruit, orange, strawberries, and pineapple. Refrigerate for
at least 2 hours. When ready to serve, fill large, stemmed red
wine glasses with ice. Fill each glass halfway with the sangria,
then top with the Cava or prosecco.

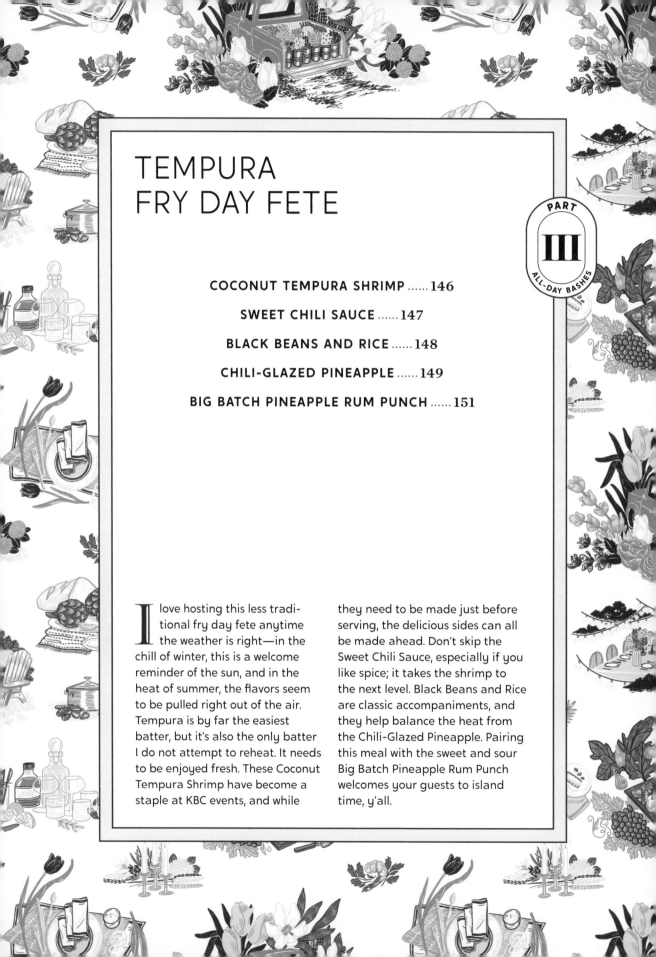

TEMPURA
FRY DAY FETE

I love hosting this less traditional fry day fete anytime the weather is right—in the chill of winter, this is a welcome reminder of the sun, and in the heat of summer, the flavors seem to be pulled right out of the air. Tempura is by far the easiest batter, but it's also the only batter I do not attempt to reheat. It needs to be enjoyed fresh. These Coconut Tempura Shrimp have become a staple at KBC events, and while they need to be made just before serving, the delicious sides can all be made ahead. Don't skip the Sweet Chili Sauce, especially if you like spice; it takes the shrimp to the next level. Black Beans and Rice are classic accompaniments, and they help balance the heat from the Chili-Glazed Pineapple. Pairing this meal with the sweet and sour Big Batch Pineapple Rum Punch welcomes your guests to island time, y'all.

Coconut Tempura Shrimp

SERVES 4 TO 6

1 cup [140 g] all-purpose flour

4 Tbsp [48 g] Tajín Clásico Seasoning

8 to 10 turns freshly ground black pepper

4 cups [945 ml] soda water

2 cups [160 g] fresh unsweetened coconut flakes

2 cups [120 g] panko

1 lb [455 g] large or jumbo shrimp, peeled and deveined but tail-on

6 cups [1.4 L] peanut or canola oil

Lime wedges, for serving

1 bunch fresh cilantro leaves, chopped, for serving

Sweet Chili Sauce (recipe follows), for serving

Line one baking sheet with parchment paper. Set a rack inside a second baking sheet.

In a medium bowl, combine the flour, 2 Tbsp of the Tajín, and the pepper, then whisk in the soda water. Do not overmix; the batter should be lumpy.

In a medium bowl, combine the coconut flakes, panko, and 1 Tbsp of Tajín.

One at a time, dip the shrimp in the tempura batter, letting any excess drip off, then dredge the shrimp in the panko mixture, pressing the mixture into the shrimp to completely coat. Place the coated shrimp in a single layer on the parchment-lined baking sheet. Freeze for 15 to 30 minutes to harden the batter and help it adhere.

In a large Dutch oven or deep fryer, heat the peanut or canola oil to 325°F [165°C].

Remove the shrimp from the freezer. Working in batches, use tongs to carefully drop the shrimp into the hot oil, being sure not to overcrowd them. Fry the shrimp, turning as needed, for 3 minutes, or until golden. Using a slotted spoon, transfer the shrimp to the rack set in the baking sheet. Repeat to fry the remaining shrimp, then sprinkle with the remaining 1 Tbsp of Tajín. Serve immediately with lime wedges, cilantro, and sweet chili sauce.

Sweet Chili Sauce

MAKES ABOUT 1 CUP [240 ML]

1 Tbsp cornstarch

2 garlic cloves, minced

½ cup [114 g] chili crunch

½ cup [170 g] honey

2 Tbsp oyster or hoisin sauce

1 tsp fish sauce

In a small pot, combine the cornstarch with just enough water to whisk it into a slurry or paste. Add the garlic, chili crunch, honey, oyster or hoisin sauce, and fish sauce and whisk to combine. Bring to a boil, then lower the heat to a simmer and cook, stirring, for 10 minutes, or until the sauce thickens. Serve warm or at room temperature alongside the coconut tempura shrimp. The sauce can be stored in an airtight container in the refrigerator for up to 6 months.

Black Beans and Rice

SERVES 4 TO 6

4 bacon slices, finely chopped

6 garlic cloves, minced

1 onion, finely chopped

1 celery stalk, finely chopped

1 jalapeño, finely chopped

Two 15 oz [425 g] cans black beans, rinsed

¼ cup [56 g] Better Than Bouillon roasted chicken base

1 cup [240 ml] coconut milk

4 bay leaves

1 tsp smoked paprika

1 tsp ground coriander

1 tsp ground cumin

Pinch of cayenne pepper

Kosher salt

Freshly ground black pepper

1 cup [200 g] long-grain white rice (I like Carolina Gold)

Lime wedges, for serving

1 bunch fresh cilantro leaves, chopped, for serving

In a large saucepan over medium heat, cook the bacon, stirring, for about 5 minutes, or until the fat is rendered. Add the garlic, onion, celery, and jalapeño and cook, stirring, for 5 minutes, or until the onion is translucent. Add the beans, chicken base, coconut milk, and enough water to cover the beans by 3 in [7.5 cm]. Add the bay leaves, smoked paprika, coriander, cumin, and cayenne and season with salt and black pepper. Bring to a boil, then lower the heat to a simmer and cook for 1 hour, adding more water as needed to keep the beans covered, or until the beans are tender. Drain and set aside.

Meanwhile, in a medium saucepan, bring the rice and 2 cups [475 ml] of water to a boil. Cover, lower the heat to a simmer, and cook for 30 minutes, or until the rice is tender and the water has been absorbed. Spread the rice on a baking sheet and refrigerate to cool.

When ready to serve, fold the cooled rice into the bean mixture and season with salt. Serve immediately, garnished with lime wedges and cilantro, or refrigerate in an airtight container for up to 3 days. Reheat in a pot over low heat or in the microwave.

Chili-Glazed Pineapple

SERVES 4 TO 6

1 pineapple, peeled, cored (optional), and cut into large rings
¼ cup [60 ml] Sweet Chili Sauce (page 147)

Set the broiler to high. Line a baking sheet with parchment paper or aluminum foil.

Arrange the pineapple rings in a single layer on the prepared baking sheet. Using a pastry brush, glaze the pineapple with the sweet chili sauce. Broil for about 5 minutes, or until the sauce caramelizes. Serve immediately.

Big Batch Pineapple Rum Punch

SERVES 4 TO 6

2 cups [475 ml] pineapple juice

1 cup [240 ml] fresh lime juice

1 cup [240 ml] dark rum

1 Tbsp Angostura bitters

4 to 6 cups [945 ml to 1.4 L] sparkling water

Pineapple leaves or wedges, for garnish

In a large pitcher, combine the pineapple juice, lime juice, rum, and bitters. Enjoy right away or cover and refrigerate for up to 1 week.

When ready to serve, add ice to glasses and fill halfway with punch, then top with sparkling water and stir. Garnish with pineapple leaves or wedges and enjoy.

PART

IV

SOUTHERN GET-TOGETHERS

Potlucks & Supper Clubs

As I mentioned in the introduction, this book is intended to inspire you to just throw the dang party. With that in mind, consider this chapter my rallying call. Designing a potluck-style meal, making casual shared plates, or cooking together with guests (a.k.a. a supper club) all take the pressure off the host and add a little extra fun to the process.

There are a few key points to ensure that a potluck feels like a party and not a PTA meeting or church picnic. First, decide what *you* want to cook. I like to cook the protein and ask guests to bring sides. Think about what components would complement your dish (perhaps an appetizer, sides—green salad, pasta salad, veggies, rolls, etc.—or a dessert). When you extend the invitation, tell guests what you're making and let them know what they can contribute with some specificity. It doesn't take that much extra work to ask for specific items, and it will

mean your guests don't have to guess. Or flip it—BYO protein is another really fun way to do a potluck, where guests bring a protein done their way, and you supply fun condiments and a delicious side or two. Either way you go, these are great ways to host a crowd. Finally, when hosting in these formats, extend the same "go forth and party" energy to your guests. If you've got the protein covered, you can even suggest that they bring takeout sides. If given the choice between them showing up or them cooking something, I'll take them showing up every time (and that's coming from a woman who dedicates her life to cooking and entertaining!). In that spirit, for each potluck in this section, I also suggest takeout sides that complement the recipes, for those who are short on time or simply don't want to strap on an apron.

Another way I love to share meal-making is by inviting friends into the kitchen. While some people love to go out to eat, I love to cook. And I really love cooking with the people I love. I consider myself a perennial student, and I also strive to be a better teacher. Cooking with my friends gives me a chance to work on both. For me, this supper club format is a chance to test out a new cookbook or to try some dishes from a culture I'm learning more about. The enjoyable memories I make while cooking with friends help me retain the recipes and techniques. The recipes in this chapter can, of course, all be made solo or for just your family, but I've indicated my favorite ways to get guests in on the action.

WING NIGHT

PART

IV

POTLUCKS & SUPPER CLUBS

Wings are the perfect party food. They have their own handle and are an ideal conduit for any sauce, spice, or condiment. They're also budget-friendly, can be made ahead and reheated, and, most importantly, they are freaking delicious, y'all. I like to serve all three versions together to offer guests some variety, but feel free to make just one—either way, you can't go wrong!

Suggested Potluck Sides

- Potato Salad
- "Dab" Salads (page 72)
- Slaw

Tandoori Wings

SERVES 4 TO 6

½ cup [120 g] plain yogurt

Juice of 1 lemon

2 tsp tomato paste

1 tsp garlic powder

1 tsp onion powder

1 tsp ground coriander

1 tsp ground cumin

1 tsp paprika

½ tsp freshly ground black pepper

¼ tsp ground ginger

¼ tsp ground cardamom

3 lbs [1.4 kg] chicken wings, rinsed and patted dry

1 lime, cut into wedges, for serving

Fresh cilantro, for garnish

In a medium bowl, whisk together the yogurt, lemon juice, tomato paste, garlic powder, onion powder, coriander, cumin, paprika, pepper, ginger, and cardamom. Add the chicken wings and toss to coat. Cover and refrigerate for at least 2 hours or up to overnight.

When ready to cook, preheat the oven to 450°F [230°C]. Line a baking sheet with parchment paper.

Spread the wings in a single layer on the prepared baking sheet and bake for 15 to 20 minutes, or until golden brown and cooked through and the internal temperature reaches 165°F [74°C]. Cool for 10 minutes, then squeeze the lime wedges over the top, sprinkle with cilantro, and serve. Alternatively, let the wings cool completely and store in an airtight container in the refrigerator for up to 3 days; reheat in a 450°F [230°C] oven for 5 minutes, or until warm.

Honey Piri-Piri Wings

SERVES 4 TO 6

½ cup [105 g] garlic ghee, melted

6 garlic cloves, thinly sliced

1 tsp garlic powder

1 tsp smoked paprika

1 tsp dried oregano

Pinch of red pepper flakes

¼ cup [85 g] honey, plus 1 tsp for marinating

3 lbs [1.4 kg] chicken wings, rinsed and patted dry

3 lemons

¾ cup [180 ml] piri-piri sauce

1 tsp kosher salt

1 tsp freshly ground black pepper

1 lime, cut into wedges

Fresh cilantro, for garnish

Fresh basil, for garnish

In a medium bowl, whisk together the ghee, garlic, garlic powder, smoked paprika, oregano, red pepper flakes, and 1 tsp of honey. Add the chicken and toss to coat. Cover and refrigerate for at least 1 hour or up to 3 days.

Meanwhile, squeeze the juice from 2 of the lemons into a small bowl, then whisk in the remaining ¼ cup [85 g] of honey, the piri-piri sauce, salt, and black pepper. Set aside.

When ready to cook, preheat the oven to 450°F [230°C]. Line a baking sheet with parchment paper.

Spread the wings in a single layer on the prepared baking sheet and bake for 10 minutes, or until golden brown. Leave the oven on.

Using a pastry brush, glaze the wings with the piri-piri sauce mixture. Bake the wings for 5 to 10 more minutes, or until sticky and glazed and the internal temperature reaches 165°F [74°C]. Cool for 10 minutes, then squeeze the lime wedges over the top, sprinkle with cilantro and basil, and serve. Alternatively, let the wings cool completely and store in an airtight container in the refrigerator for up to 3 days; reheat in a 450°F [230°C] oven for 5 minutes, or until warm.

Za'atar Wings with Harissa Sauce

SERVES 4 TO 6

½ cup [120 ml] olive oil

Zest and juice of 1 lemon

Zest and juice of 1 orange

¼ cup [25 g] za'atar

1 Tbsp kosher salt

1 tsp dried rosemary

1 tsp dried thyme

8 to 10 turns freshly ground black pepper

3 lbs [1.4 kg] chicken wings, rinsed and patted dry

½ cup [20 g] chopped fresh flat-leaf parsley, for garnish

Harissa Sauce (recipe follows), for serving

In a medium bowl, whisk together the olive oil, lemon zest and juice, orange zest and juice, za'atar, salt, rosemary, thyme, and pepper. Add the chicken and toss to coat. Cover and refrigerate for at least 1 hour or up to 3 days.

When ready to cook, preheat the oven to 450°F [230°C]. Line a baking sheet with parchment paper. Spread the wings in a single layer on the prepared baking sheet and bake for 15 to 20 minutes, or until golden brown and the internal temperature reaches 165°F [74°C]. Cool for 10 minutes, then sprinkle with parsley and serve with the harissa sauce. Store the cooled leftovers in an airtight container in the refrigerator for up to 3 days; reheat in a 450°F [230°C] oven for 5 minutes, or until warm.

Harissa Sauce

MAKES 1 CUP [227 G]

½ cup [150 g] tahini

½ cup [120 g] Greek yogurt

Zest and juice of 1 lemon

2 garlic cloves, minced

2 tsp harissa paste

1 tsp kosher salt

½ tsp ground sumac

In a medium bowl, whisk together the ingredients. Store in an airtight container in the refrigerator for up to 3 days.

BYO STEAK NIGHT

When it comes to steak, everyone has a personal preference on cut, seasoning, marinade, and temperature, which is great, but I don't like feeling like I'm a short-order cook in my own home. Been there, done that! BYO steak allows guests to make all of these decisions on their own, and when they arrive, we share the grill to cook their steaks to perfection. To make it feel steak house special, I love making compound butter for guests to add some extra-rich finish and flavor. (Bonus: Compound butter elevates anything you use it on—shrimp, fish, chicken, grilled asparagus, or roasted potatoes—so making extra and storing some in the freezer is a no-brainer.)

Because I'm a sucker for classics with a twist, I like to make a Grilled Southern Caesar Salad, Twice-Baked Potatoes, and Carnegie Deli–Inspired Cheesecake for this gathering. It's your choice whether you make them all yourself, farm them out potluck-style, or go rogue and create your own sides.

Suggested Potluck Sides

- Mashed potatoes
- Roasted sweet potatoes
- Grilled asparagus
- Creamed spinach
- Sautéed mushrooms
- A hearty salad from one of your favorite local spots

Steak Oscar

SERVES 4 TO 6

Foolproof Caterers' Hollandaise

6 large egg yolks

2 Tbsp fresh lemon juice

Kosher salt

3 cups [678 g] unsalted butter, melted and cooled to warm

Steaks of your guests' choosing (everyone should bring their favorite cut!), cooked to their liking

Grilled Asparagus

3 lb [1.4 kg] asparagus

¼ cup [60 ml] olive oil

Kosher salt

Freshly ground black pepper

3 lb [1.4 kg] jumbo lump crabmeat (or more—more is more for me when it comes to crab!)
Dash of cayenne pepper, for garnish

To make the foolproof caterers' hollandaise: Place the egg yolks, lemon juice, 2 Tbsp of water, and a pinch of salt in a tall cup or a blender. Using a blender or in the cup of an immersion blender, gradually add the warm butter in a very fine, slow drizzle with the blender running. Continue blending until all the butter is added and the ingredients emulsify, creating a creamy, pale yellow sauce that is thick enough to coat the back of a spoon. If it's too thick, gradually blend in warm water, 1 Tbsp at a time, until the consistency is right. Serve immediately or keep warm in a double boiler or small lidded heatproof bowl set over a pot of warm water. If the sauce breaks, reblend.

While your guests enjoy grilling steaks to their liking, grill the asparagus: Toss the asparagus in the olive oil and season with salt and black pepper. Throw the asparagus on the grill, next to the steaks, and grill for roughly 3 minutes—do not overcook! Asparagus should never bend and should always stand tall like a tree.

To serve: On individual plates or a large platter, lay a bed of asparagus down and place the cooked steak on top. Arrange the crabmeat on top of the steak, drizzle with the hollandaise, sprinkle with the cayenne, and enjoy immediately.

Compound Butter, Three Ways

No. One

Garlic and Herbes de Provence Compound Butter

SERVES 6 TO 8

½ cup [113 g] unsalted butter, at room temperature

4 garlic cloves, minced

2 Tbsp herbes de Provence

1 Tbsp minced shallots

1 Tbsp minced fresh chives

½ tsp kosher salt

8 to 10 turns freshly ground black pepper

In a medium bowl, mash together the butter, garlic, herbes de Provence, shallots, chives, salt, and pepper. Spoon the butter onto a piece of parchment paper or plastic wrap, roll it into a log about 2 to 3 in [5 to 7.5 cm] in diameter, and wrap tightly. Chill for at least 3 hours in the refrigerator or 1 hour in the freezer before using, or store in the freezer for up to 6 months.

No. Two

Truffle Compound Butter

SERVES 6 TO 8

½ cup [113 g] unsalted butter, at room temperature

2 Tbsp fresh or jarred grated white or black truffles

½ tsp truffle salt

8 to 10 turns freshly ground black pepper

In a medium bowl, mash together the butter, truffles, truffle salt, and pepper. Spoon the butter onto a piece of parchment paper or plastic wrap, roll it into a log about 2 to 3 in [5 to 7.5 cm] in diameter, and wrap tightly. Chill for at least 3 hours in the refrigerator or 1 hour in the freezer before using, or store in the freezer for up to 6 months.

No. Three

Umami Compound Butter

SERVES 6 TO 8

½ cup [113 g] unsalted butter, at room temperature

1 Tbsp mushroom powder

1 Tbsp soy sauce

1 tsp Worcestershire sauce

1 tsp oyster sauce

3 or 4 drops fish sauce

8 to 10 turns freshly ground black pepper

In a medium bowl, mash together the butter, mushroom powder, soy sauce, Worcestershire sauce, oyster sauce, fish sauce, and pepper. Spoon the butter onto a piece of parchment paper or plastic wrap, roll it into a log about 2 to 3 in [5 to 7.5 cm] in diameter, and wrap tightly. Chill for at least 3 hours in the refrigerator or 1 hour in the freezer before using, or store in the freezer for up to 6 months.

Grilled Southern Caesar Salad

SERVES 4 TO 6

Dressing

1 oz [30 g] smoked trout or anchovies

2 garlic cloves

2 large egg yolks

Zest and juice of 1 lemon

1 tsp Dijon mustard

½ cup [120 ml] vegetable or canola oil

3 Tbsp grated Parmesan cheese

10 to 15 turns freshly ground black pepper

Croutons

1 loaf French bread, ripped into
bite-size pieces

2 cups [120 g] panko

2 Tbsp olive oil

Salad

8 romaine hearts

2 Tbsp olive oil

Kosher salt

1 cup [30 g] freshly grated Parmesan cheese

1 cup [70 g] freshly shaved Parmesan cheese

1 lemon, cut into wedges, for garnish

Freshly ground black pepper

To make the dressing: In a food processor, combine the trout, garlic, egg yolks, lemon zest and juice, and mustard. Pulse until smooth. With the blender on high speed, gradually add the vegetable or canola oil in a very fine, slow drizzle. Continue blending until all the oil is added and the dressing is thick. Add the Parmesan and pepper and pulse to incorporate. If the dressing is too thick, gradually blend in room-temperature water, 1 Tbsp at a time, until the consistency is right. It should be thin enough to be drizzled. The dressing can be made ahead and stored in an airtight container in the refrigerator for up to 1 week.

To make the croutons: Preheat the oven to 350°F [180°C].

In a large bowl, combine the bread pieces, panko, olive oil, and 2 Tbsp of the dressing and toss to fully coat the bread. Spread the bread in a single layer on one or two baking sheets and bake for 15 to 20 minutes, or until golden and crunchy. These can be made ahead and stored in an airtight container in the pantry for up to 3 days.

To make the salad: Preheat the grill to 350 to 400°F [180 to 200°C].

Rip the leaves from five of the romaine hearts into big pieces and set aside. Cut the remaining three romaine hearts lengthwise in half. Drizzle the olive oil over the halved romaine, then sprinkle with salt. Set the halved romaine, cut-side down, directly on the grill racks and grill, flipping, for 2 to 5 minutes total, or just until grill marks appear. Alternatively, place a large skillet or grill pan on the stovetop over high heat and cook the romaine, flipping, until sear marks appear.

On a large platter or in a large bowl, combine the grilled romaine, ripped romaine, croutons, grated and shaved Parmesan, and about ½ cup [120 ml] of the dressing. Toss to coat, adding more dressing, about ½ cup [120 ml] at a time, just until the salad is lightly coated. Squeeze the lemon over the top, season with pepper, and enjoy immediately.

Twice-Baked Potatoes

MAKES 8 POTATO HALVES; SERVES 4 TO 8

4 large russet potatoes

1 cup [226 g] unsalted butter, cubed, at room temperature

Kosher salt

½ cup [120 g] sour cream

3 cups [240 g] freshly grated Cheddar cheese

½ cup [120 ml] heavy cream

½ tsp ground white pepper

Freshly ground black pepper

1 bunch green onions, green and white parts, minced

Preheat the oven to 400°F [200°C]. Line a baking sheet with parchment paper.

In a large bowl, toss the potatoes with 2 Tbsp of the butter and about 1 Tbsp of salt. Spread the potatoes evenly on the prepared baking sheet and roast for about 1 hour, or until the potato skins are crispy and the potatoes can be pierced easily with a fork. Remove the potatoes from the oven and let cool for 15 to 20 minutes, or until cool enough to handle.

Cut the potatoes lengthwise in half. Scoop out the potatoes, leaving about ⅛ in [3 mm] of cooked potato on the skin, and put the flesh in a medium bowl or the bowl of a stand mixer fitted with the paddle attachment. Add the remaining ¾ cup plus 2 Tbsp [200 g] of butter, the sour cream, and 1 cup [80 g] of the Cheddar and use a wooden spoon or the paddle to beat until incorporated. Gradually start adding the heavy cream, 1 Tbsp at a time, and beat until the potatoes are smooth and just mixed together—do not add too much cream or it will make the potato mixture too thin. Add the white pepper and season with salt and black pepper. Evenly divide the potato mixture among the potato skins, then top with the remaining Cheddar. Bake for 10 minutes, or until the cheese is golden and bubbling. Let cool slightly, then garnish with green onions and serve. Alternatively, you can cover and refrigerate the filled and topped potatoes for up to 3 days or wrap them in aluminum foil or plastic wrap and freeze for up to 3 months. Thaw as needed and let them come to room temperature before baking at 400°F [200°C] for 10 minutes.

Carnegie Deli–Inspired Cheesecake

SERVES 12 TO 16

Crust

3 cups [420 g] all-purpose flour

1½ cups [300 g] granulated sugar

1 Tbsp vanilla extract

1 Tbsp baking powder

1 tsp kosher salt

1½ cups [339 g] unsalted butter, melted

Filling

1 lb [455 g] whole milk ricotta, at room temperature (and drained, if at all wet)

8 oz [230 g] full-fat cream cheese, at room temperature

1 cup [200 g] granulated sugar

1 Tbsp cornstarch

4 large eggs, at room temperature

Zest and juice of 1 lemon

2 tsp vanilla extract or 1 Tbsp vanilla bean paste

½ tsp kosher salt

Orange slices, for garnish

Thinly sliced lemon peel, for garnish

To make the crust: Preheat the oven to 350°F [180°C]. Butter a 9 in [23 cm] springform pan with sides at least 3 in [7.5 cm] high. Wrap the entire exterior of the pan in a double layer of aluminum foil, creating a seal to keep water out during the water bath step.

In a medium bowl, whisk together the flour, sugar, vanilla, baking powder, and salt. Pour the melted butter over the flour mixture, then stir with your fingers until the butter is fully incorporated. Use your fingers to press the crust mixture into the bottom and halfway up the sides of the springform pan. Don't worry if the sides are not perfectly even or if the crumbs reach above or below the halfway point on the sides of the pan—it's meant to be organic.

Freeze for 5 to 15 minutes or wrap in a double layer of aluminum foil or plastic wrap and freeze for up to 2 months.

Set the springform pan on a baking sheet and bake for 10 minutes, or until golden. Set the crust aside to cool while you make the filling.   **cont.**

171

To make the filling: Lower the oven temperature to 325°F [165°C]. Bring a pot or kettle filled with water to a boil.

In the bowl of a stand mixer fitted with the paddle attachment, combine the ricotta, cream cheese, sugar, and cornstarch and beat on high speed, scraping down the sides of the bowl as needed, for about 5 minutes, or until completely smooth and creamy. With the mixer on low speed, add the eggs, one at a time, followed by the lemon zest and juice, vanilla, and salt. Continue beating, scraping down the sides of bowl as needed, for 3 to 5 more minutes, or until completely smooth.

Give the batter a few stirs with a rubber spatula, just to make sure that nothing has been left unmixed at the bottom of the bowl, then pour it into the crust in the springform pan. Put the springform pan flat in a roasting pan, then set the roasting pan in the oven. Carefully pour enough of the boiling water into the roasting pan to come halfway up the sides of the springform pan.

Bake for 1½ to 2 hours, or until the cheesecake rises just above the rim of the pan and is lightly browned; it may have a small crack or two on top. Carefully remove the roasting pan from the oven and let the cheesecake stand in the water bath at room temperature for 1 hour.

After 1 hour, carefully lift the springform pan out of the roasting pan and remove the foil. Let the cheesecake stand at room temperature until cool to the touch, then loosely cover and refrigerate for at least 4 hours but preferably overnight.

When ready to serve, grab a pitcher filled with hot or boiling water, a long knife, a dish towel, and a blow-dryer. With the dryer on low heat, blow the sides of the springform pan all the way around for about 2 minutes. This will melt the butter ever so slightly, making it easy for the cake to release. Remove the ring to release the cheesecake from the pan. Arrange the orange slices and lemon peels around the top edge of the cake. To cut, dip the knife in hot water, shake it slightly to remove any excess water, and then slice. Wipe the knife clean on the towel after each cut and dip it in hot water before each new cut. The cheesecake can be well wrapped and refrigerated for up to 1 week or frozen for up to 2 months.

BYO BURGER NIGHT

Burgers are like steaks in that there are a million ways to prep them, and they are all good. A BYO burger night is a fun way to try some new variations and swap "family secrets" for cooking the best burger. Since your guests bring their own burger patties, you get to indulge in my favorite part of these nights—building the toppings bar, including *all* the sauces, coming up with creative additions, and building a milkshake bar. To complement the burgers, salads are a must, especially my Orzo Pasta Salad. Here are a couple other sides to round out your menu. They can be homemade, either by you or your guests, or prepared by your favorite deli or barbecue shack.

Suggested Potluck Sides

- Slaw, baked beans, mac & cheese, potato salad
- Salad and breadsticks from Olive Garden (they are freaking delicious)
- Pasta, couscous, or quinoa salad

Building *the* Best Burger Bar

It's always all about the bar, isn't it? Without too much effort, you can offer great toppings that create such a wow factor on your burger bar. You'd never pull out all the stops like this for a weeknight burger, so it's a treat to go ahead and lay it all out. Take a little time to arrange the veggies, pull out the pretty serveware, and you'll end up with a pretty eye-catching table too!

VEGGIES

- [ ] Lettuce (I like to have a variety, like Bibb, arugula, and romaine)
- [ ] Sautéed mushrooms
- [ ] Sautéed onions and peppers
- [ ] Sliced jalapeños
- [ ] Thickly sliced tomatoes
- [ ] Thinly sliced white and red onions

PROTEINS & DAIRY

- [ ] Bacon
- [ ] Fried eggs
- [ ] Pepper jack, Cheddar, American, smoked Gouda, and Gorgonzola cheeses

CONDIMENTS

- [ ] Barbecue sauce
- [ ] Buffalo sauce
- [ ] Dijon, yellow, and whole-grain mustards
- [ ] Hot sauce
- [ ] Ketchup
- [ ] Mayonnaise

MISCELLANEOUS

- [ ] Olives
- [ ] Potato chips
- [ ] Relish
- [ ] Sliced pickles

The Three Best Burger Sauces

No. One
Horseradish Mustard
MAKES 2 CUPS [480 G]

2 cups [480 g] mayonnaise

2 Tbsp freshly grated or prepared horseradish

2 Tbsp whole-grain mustard

1 tsp garlic powder

1 tsp onion powder

In a medium bowl, whisk together the mayonnaise, horseradish, mustard, garlic powder, and onion powder. Use immediately or refrigerate in an airtight container for up to 3 months.

No. Two
Bacon Onion Jam
MAKES 2 CUPS [480 G]

1 lb [455 g] bacon, finely chopped

1 onion, chopped

2 garlic cloves, minced

½ cup [120 ml] apple cider vinegar

Pinch of red pepper flakes

½ cup [170 g] honey

In a skillet, cook the bacon over low heat for about 15 minutes, or until the fat renders and the bacon is crispy. Transfer the bacon to a paper towel–lined plate or cooling rack. Pour off most of the fat from the pan, then add the onion and garlic and cook for

5 minutes, or until translucent. Add the bacon, vinegar, red pepper flakes, honey, and ½ cup [120 ml] of water and simmer until thick and syrupy, about 45 minutes. Remove from the heat and let cool, then leave as is or purée in a food processor until smooth. Use immediately or refrigerate in an airtight container for up to 3 months.

No. Three
"Welcome to Good Burger, Home of the Good Burger" Sauce
MAKES 2 CUPS [480 G]

½ cup [120 g] mayonnaise

5 kosher dill pickles, finely chopped

1 Tbsp ketchup

1 Tbsp yellow mustard

1 tsp garlic powder

1 tsp onion powder

½ tsp Worcestershire sauce

¼ tsp paprika

Pinch of cayenne pepper

In a medium bowl, whisk together the mayonnaise, pickles, ketchup, mustard, garlic powder, onion powder, Worcestershire sauce, paprika, and cayenne. Use immediately or refrigerate in an airtight container for up to 3 months.

The Best Burger Side: Orzo Pasta Salad

SERVES 4 TO 6

4 cups [945 ml] chicken broth

2 cups [200 g] orzo

Kosher salt

One 15 oz [425 g] can chickpeas, drained and rinsed

One 14 oz [400 g] can hearts of palm, drained and chopped

2 cups [320 g] grape, cherry, or teardrop tomatoes, halved

1 small red onion, finely chopped

½ cup [70 g] pitted and chopped Kalamata olives

½ cup [60 g] crumbled feta

2 garlic cloves, minced

½ cup [20 g] chopped fresh basil

½ cup [20 g] chopped fresh flat-leaf parsley

1 tsp chopped fresh or dried oregano

1 cup [240 ml] olive oil

¼ cup [60 ml] red wine vinegar

¼ cup [60 ml] balsamic vinegar

2 Tbsp mayonnaise

1 tsp honey

Freshly ground black pepper

In a medium pot, bring the broth to a boil. Add the orzo and 1 Tbsp of salt and cook for 10 to 15 minutes, or until al dente. Drain the orzo, then transfer to a medium bowl and add the chickpeas, hearts of palm, tomatoes, red onion, olives, feta, and garlic. Sprinkle with the basil, parsley, and oregano and toss to combine.

In a small bowl, whisk together the olive oil, red wine vinegar, balsamic vinegar, mayonnaise, and honey. Season with salt and pepper. Pour the dressing over the salad, toss to coat, and season with salt. Serve immediately or refrigerate in an airtight container for up to 3 days.

Milkshake Bar

Burgers and milkshakes are a perfect retro pairing, and a milkshake bar is such a joyous, simple way to delight your guests. There literally is no prep (hallelujah!), just some setup. As a bonus, if you like, you can add a spiked milkshake element. Throw on your poodle skirt or leather jacket and get the jukebox playing.

EQUIPMENT & SUPPLIES

- ☐ Blender and/or immersion blender
- ☐ Decanter or glass carafe for milk or cream
- ☐ Large ice bucket
- ☐ Milkshake cups or glasses
- ☐ Milkshake straws
- ☐ Small jars or bowls for toppings
- ☐ Suggested recipe cards (optional)

ICE CREAM & TOPPINGS

- ☐ Gallons of vanilla, chocolate, strawberry, and coffee ice cream, arranged in a large ice bucket filled with ice
- ☐ Milk or cream in a decanter, pitcher, or glass jug in the ice bucket (do not fill to the brim and leave room to avoid spilling if using a vessel without a lid)
- ☐ **Liquor:** brandy, Fireball Cinnamon Whisky, Kahlúa, rum, whiskey
- ☐ **Toppings:** bananas, bourbon cherries, caramel sauce, chocolate chips, chocolate sauce, cinnamon, cream of coconut, crushed Oreo cookies, crushed vanilla wafers, maraschino cherries, sprinkles, whipped cream

MILKSHAKE RECIPES

Each of these recipes makes one milkshake. If you don't have an immersion blender, make these shakes in a blender, transfer to the milkshake cups, then add the toppings.

• BANANAS FOSTER •

Using a spoon, mash 1 banana in the bottom of a milkshake cup, then add 4 scoops of vanilla ice cream, 1 Tbsp of caramel sauce, and 2 shots of rum (or more if you'd like). While blending, add milk, 2 Tbsp at a time, until you reach the desired consistency. Top with whipped cream, a drizzle of caramel sauce, and vanilla wafer crumbles.

• RED-EYE COFFEE •

In a milkshake cup, combine 4 scoops of coffee ice cream, 1 Tbsp of chocolate sauce, and 2 shots of Kahlúa. While blending, add milk, 2 Tbsp at a time, until you reach the desired consistency. Top with whipped cream, a drizzle of chocolate sauce, and a maraschino cherry.

• BRANDY FREEZE •

In a milkshake cup, combine 4 scoops of vanilla ice cream, 1 Tbsp of chocolate sauce, and 2 shots of brandy. While blending, add milk, 2 Tbsp at a time, until you reach the desired consistency. Top with whipped cream, if desired.

• MEXICAN CHOCOLATE •

In a milkshake cup, combine 4 scoops of chocolate ice cream, 2 Tbsp of chocolate sauce, and 2 shots of Fireball. While blending, add milk, 2 Tbsp at a time, until you reach the desired consistency. Top with whipped cream, a drizzle of chocolate sauce, and a dash of cinnamon.

STREET TACO SUPPER CLUB

There is no occasion when I'm gonna say no to a street taco, and I've found that my feelings seem to be shared by most. Street tacos are typically served in pairs and feature fresh, hot tortillas filled with meat, raw onions, and cilantro, with a side of salsa and lime. They are bright, light, simple, and clean yet also complex in flavor and spice—a delicious snapshot of authentic Mexican cuisine. When I serve this menu, I like to have everything cooked and ready to serve ahead of time (and being kept warm in a 250°F [120°C] oven if needed). I also prepare the tortilla dough in advance and then, when my guests arrive, I show them how to roll the tortillas and we get cooking and assembling!

Round this menu out with margaritas from my first book, *Southern Grit*, or make a batch of Mexican mules (see page 93).

Suggested Potluck Sides and Desserts:

- Rice and beans
- Green salad
- Churros picked up from your favorite Mexican restaurant with chocolate sauce from the grocery store. (If your local restaurant doesn't have churros, look for frozen ones at the grocery store.) To heat them, simply bake on a parchment paper–lined sheet tray in a 450°F [230°C] oven for 5 to 8 minutes, or until crispy.

Tortillas on the Fly

SERVES 8 TO 10

3¼ cups [490 g] all-purpose flour
½ cup [90 g] shortening or lard

Put the flour in a medium bowl, then gradually add the shortening or lard, one spoonful at a time, and rub between your fingers to blend the flour and fat and create a loose paste. Add 1 cup [240 ml] of hot water to the flour mixture and knead the mixture until it forms a dough. If the dough is not coming together, add more hot water, 1 Tbsp at a time. If the dough appears sticky or too wet, add more flour, 1 Tbsp at a time, kneading with your hands until the dough has a consistency similar to Play-Doh. Transfer the dough to a clean work surface and knead for 3 to 5 minutes, or until smooth and shiny. Shape the dough into a ball and return it to the bowl. Cover the bowl with a damp paper towel and let stand at room temperature for at least 2 hours or up to all day. When I'm having guests over at night, I like to make the dough in the morning, but you can make it the night before, wrap it airtight, and refrigerate it. In the morning, remove the dough from the refrigerator, unwrap it, and follow the directions below.

After at least 2 hours, on a clean work surface, knead the dough for 2 to 3 minutes to resoften. Roll the dough into a long snake-like shape and cut it crosswise into 1½ to 2 in [4 to 5 cm] pieces. Lightly flour the work surface, then use the palm of your hand to press each piece of dough into a 6 to 8 in [15 to 20 cm] diameter circle that's about ⅛ in [3 mm] thick, or use a lined tortilla press.

Heat an electric griddle to 375°F [190°C] or place a skillet over medium-low heat. (I prefer an electric griddle for tortillas because the heat is uniform over the entire surface.) Place 3 or 4 tortillas on the hot griddle or skillet and cook, flipping, for 15 to 20 seconds on each side, or until bubbling, light brown, and speckled. Repeat to cook the remaining tortillas. Wrap finished tortillas in a tea towel to keep warm for serving.

Citrus-Marinated Flank Steak (Carne Asada)

SERVES 4 TO 6

Juice of 1 orange (about ¼ cup [60 ml] juice)

Juice of 2 limes (about ¼ cup [60 ml] juice)

¼ cup [60 ml] olive oil

¼ cup [60 ml] Worcestershire sauce

1 onion, thinly sliced

6 garlic cloves, minced

1 jalapeño, seeded and minced

½ cup [20 g] fresh cilantro, chopped

1 tsp peppercorns

1 tsp Ancho chile powder

½ tsp coriander seeds

½ tsp cumin seeds

2 lbs [910 g] flank, flap, or skirt steak

In a shallow dish, whisk together the orange juice, lime juice, olive oil, Worcestershire sauce, onion, garlic, jalapeño, cilantro, peppercorns, chile powder, coriander, and cumin. Add the steak, turning to coat it in the marinade, then cover the dish and refrigerate for at least 1 hour but no more than 2 hours—marinating too long breaks down the muscle fibers, making for mushy steak.

When ready to cook, remove the steak from marinade and pat it dry with a paper towel; reserve the marinade.

Place a large skillet or grill pan over medium heat. Add the steak and cook, flipping, for 3 to 4 minutes on each side for medium-rare, 4 to 5 minutes on each side for medium, and 6 to 7 minutes on each side for well-done. Let rest on a cutting board for 15 minutes.

While the meat is resting, pour the reserved marinade into a medium saucepan. Bring to a rolling boil over high heat and continue boiling until thick and reduced by half. Strain.

Cut the steak against the grain (to ensure it's tender) into very thin pieces. Drizzle with the steak sauce and enjoy.

Salsa, Three Ways

No. One
Salsa Taquera

MAKES 4 CUPS [1 KG]

3 to 6 dried chiles de árbol

1 lb [455 g] Roma tomatoes, chopped

1 lb [455 g] tomatillos, husked, rinsed, and halved

1 onion, chopped

2 jalapeños, stemmed (and seeded for less heat)

2 garlic cloves, peeled

Kosher salt

In a large cast-iron skillet, toast the chiles over medium-high heat until lightly toasted and fragrant, about 1 minute. Remove from the skillet. Add the tomatoes, tomatillos, onion, jalapeños, and garlic to the skillet and cook, stirring frequently, for 10 minutes, or until slightly charred. Add the tomato mixture and chiles to a blender or food processor and blend until smooth. Season with salt. Store in an airtight container in the refrigerator for up to 1 week.

No. Two
Pico de Gallo

MAKES 2 CUPS [480 G]

1 lb [455 g] ripe tomatoes, finely chopped

1 cup [140 g] minced red onion

3 jalapeños or serrano chiles, seeded and chopped

¼ cup [10 g] chopped fresh cilantro

Juice of 1 lime

Kosher salt

In a medium bowl, toss together the tomatoes, red onion, chiles, cilantro, and lime juice. Season with salt. Let stand at room temperature for 30 minutes to develop the flavors or refrigerate in an airtight container for up to 1 week.

No. Three
Salsa Verde

MAKES 2 CUPS [520 G]

1 lb [455 g] tomatillos, husked, rinsed, and halved

1 onion, chopped

3 jalapeños or serrano chiles, seeded and chopped

2 garlic cloves, peeled

1 bunch fresh cilantro, leaves chopped

Juice of 1 lime

Kosher salt

Set the broiler to its highest setting, ideally 500°F [260°C]. Line a baking sheet with aluminum foil. Arrange the tomatillos, stem-side down, on the prepared baking sheet. Broil for 5 minutes, or until charred. Transfer the tomatillos and any juices to a blender or food processor. Add the onion, chiles, garlic, cilantro, and lime juice and blend until smooth. Season with salt. Let stand at room temperature for 30 minutes to develop the flavors or refrigerate in an airtight container for up to 1 week.

Guacamole

SERVES 4 TO 6

4 or 5 avocados, halved, pitted, and peeled

½ cup Pico de Gallo (opposite), Salsa Verde (opposite), or Salsa Taquera (opposite)

Juice of 1 lime

1 to 3 Tbsp Tajín Clásico Seasoning

Place the avocados in a large bowl and coarsely mash them. Add the salsa, lime juice, and Tajín and fold until well incorporated. Enjoy immediately with fried tortilla chips or use as a condiment for tacos.

NOTE

I don't recommend making guacamole the day before, but you can make it a few hours ahead. Press a piece of parchment paper or plastic wrap directly on the surface of the guacamole to prevent browning and refrigerate until ready to serve.

MEZZE MEAL

PART

IV

POTLUCKS & SUPPER CLUBS

Mezze is a style of dining in the Mediterranean and Middle East that has (thankfully!) become popular in the States and there's not a single wonder why. It's essentially the dip table of everyone's dreams, plus meats and all the delicious small plates and bites you could ever imagine. In other words, there's somethin' for everyone.

This is one of my favorite spreads to throw together and the reaction is always the same: *When can we do this again?* I am including a lot of recipes here, because I really want y'all to understand that this is meant to be a S P R E A D.

I love inviting friends to join in preparing this menu. As the host, I make the pita dough ahead of time, cook the meat, and have everything else cooked and in serving dishes (and being kept warm in a 250°F [120°C] oven if needed). Once your helpers (guests) arrive, show them how to roll and cook the pitas and form the koftas.

Suggested Potluck Sides:

- Baba ghanoush
- Tabbouleh
- Dolmas
- Falafel
- Olives

Crunchy Chickpeas

MAKES 3 CUPS [450 G]

Two 15 oz [425 g] cans chickpeas, drained, rinsed, and patted dry

¼ cup [60 ml] olive oil

Zest and juice of 1 lemon

1 Tbsp kosher salt

2 tsp za'atar

1 tsp ground sumac

1 tsp ground harissa

½ tsp smoked paprika

Preheat the oven to 400°F [200°C]. Line one or two baking sheets with parchment paper.

In a large bowl, combine the chickpeas with the olive oil, lemon zest and juice, salt, za'atar, sumac, harissa, and paprika and toss to coat. Spread the chickpeas in a single layer on the prepared baking sheets. Roast, shaking the baking sheet and stirring the chickpeas every 10 minutes, for 30 to 40 minutes total, or until golden and crispy. Store in an airtight container for up to 3 days.

Dip Trio

No. One
Tzatziki

MAKES 2 TO 3 CUPS [480 TO 720 G]

1 English cucumber, grated on a box grater

2 cups [480 g] plain Greek yogurt

1 garlic clove, grated on a Microplane or box grater

Zest and juice of 1 lemon

2 Tbsp chopped fresh chives

1 Tbsp chopped fresh dill

1 Tbsp olive oil

8 to 10 turns freshly ground black pepper

Kosher salt

In a fine-mesh sieve set over a small bowl, drain the grated cucumber, pressing and squeezing to release any excess liquid. Reserve the liquid to make Cucumber Collins (page 201). Transfer the drained cucumber to a medium bowl and add the yogurt, garlic, lemon zest and juice, chives, dill, olive oil, and pepper. Season with salt. Use immediately or refrigerate in an airtight container for up to 1 week.

No. Two
Whipped Feta

SERVES 4 TO 6

½ cup [120 ml] olive oil, plus more for serving

10 oz [285 g] feta

4 oz [115 g] cream cheese, at room temperature

Zest and juice of 2 lemons

2 tsp honey

¼ cup [30 g] pine nuts, toasted

2 Tbsp chopped fresh flat-leaf parsley

2 Tbsp chopped fresh mint

In the bowl of a stand mixer fitted with the whisk attachment or in a food processor, combine the olive oil, feta, cream cheese, lemon juice, and 1 tsp of the honey. Mix or process, scraping down the bowl regularly, for 3 to 5 minutes, or until light and whipped. Drizzle with 2 Tbsp of olive oil and the remaining 1 tsp of honey. Sprinkle with the lemon zest, pine nuts, parsley, and mint and serve immediately, or refrigerate, without the garnishes, in an airtight container for up to 3 days. Re-whip and add garnishes before serving.   cont.

No. Three
Butter Bean Hummus

SERVES 4 TO 6

4 cups [945 ml] chicken stock

2 cups [320 g] fresh or frozen butter beans or lima beans

½ onion, roughly chopped

2 Tbsp unsalted butter

1 Tbsp kosher salt

1 tsp freshly ground black pepper

3 garlic cloves, peeled

½ cup [150 g] tahini

½ cup [120 ml] olive oil, plus more for serving

Zest and juice of 2 large lemons

¼ cup [10 g] chopped fresh flat-leaf parsley

In a medium pot, bring the stock, beans, onion, butter, salt, and pepper to a boil. Cook the beans for 30 to 45 minutes, until they are overcooked and mushy. Drain the beans, reserving the liquid, and let cool to room temperature.

In a food processor, combine the cooked beans, garlic, and tahini and process until smooth. With the processor running, gradually drizzle in the olive oil, alternating with 1 Tbsp of the reserved bean liquid. Add the lemon juice, followed by more bean liquid if the dip is too thick. Process until completely smooth. Drizzle with more olive oil and sprinkle with the lemon zest and parsley. Store in an airtight container in the refrigerator for up to three days.

HUMMUS VARIATIONS

Mix in 2 Tbsp of harissa, then top with a few Tbsp of toasted pine nuts.

Mix in 2 Tbsp of red pepper paste, then top with chickpeas and smoked paprika.

Mash an avocado with lemon juice, fresh parsley, dill, and cilantro, then add to the cooked beans.

Mash black garlic, then add to the cooked beans, drizzle with chili crunch, and garnish with fresh cilantro.

Fold in ¼ cup [57 g] of olive tapenade, a pinch of dried oregano, and 1 Tbsp of chopped preserved lemon.

Sub black-eyed peas, peanuts, chickpeas, or carrots for the butter beans or lima beans.

Homemade Pita

MAKES SIX TO EIGHT 6 IN [15 CM] ROUND PITAS

¼ cup [35 g] whole wheat flour

One ¾ oz [20 g] package active dry yeast

½ tsp granulated sugar

2¼ cups [315 g] all-purpose flour

2 Tbsp olive oil

1 tsp kosher salt

Preheat the oven as high as it will go, 450 to 500°F [230 to 260°C]. Put a pizza stone or heavy-duty baking sheet on the bottom rack of the oven. (This can also be baked in a pizza oven.)

In a medium bowl, stir together the whole wheat flour, yeast, sugar, and 1 cup [240 ml] of warm water. Let stand, uncovered, for 15 minutes. Using a wooden spoon, stir in the all-purpose flour, olive oil, and salt, pressing and folding until it resembles a shaggy dough. Turn the dough out onto a lightly floured work surface and knead for 3 to 5 minutes, or until smooth. Return the dough to the bowl, lightly cover the bowl with a tea towel, and let rest in a warm space (74 to 80°F [23 to 27°C] is ideal) for about 1 hour, or until doubled in size.

Punch down the dough, then form it into 6 to 8 evenly sized balls. Cover the dough balls with the tea towel and let rest for 10 more minutes. Use a rolling pin to roll out one ball of dough into a disk about ⅛ in [3 mm] thick. Repeat to roll out the remaining balls of dough. Keep the dough covered while you work.

Put one or two disks of dough on the preheated baking sheet in the oven and bake for 2 to 3 minutes, or until they puff up. Flip the pita over and bake for 1 more minute. Remove the pita from the oven, then immediately wrap them in a towel and leave on the counter. Repeat to bake the remaining pita, stacking one on top of another inside the towel. Enjoy immediately or cool and refrigerate in an airtight container for up to 5 days or freeze for up to 3 months, thawing before use. Reheat in a 400°F [200°C] oven for just a few minutes.

Fattoush

SERVES 4 TO 6

4 Homemade Pitas (page 195) or store-bought, torn into bite-size pieces

10 Tbsp [150 ml] olive oil

Kosher salt

2 tomatoes, diced

1 English cucumber, diced

1 bunch green onions, green and white parts, finely chopped

2 garlic cloves, minced

1 bunch fresh flat-leaf parsley, leaves chopped

4 to 6 fresh mint leaves, chopped

Zest and juice of 1 lemon

Pinch of ground coriander

Preheat the oven to 400°F [200°C].

In a medium bowl, toss the pita pieces with 2 Tbsp of the olive oil and a big pinch of salt. Spread in a single layer on a baking sheet and bake, stirring a few times, for 10 minutes, or until golden, crunchy, and evenly toasted. Let cool.

Meanwhile, in a medium bowl, toss together the tomatoes, cucumber, green onions, garlic, parsley, mint, lemon zest and juice, the remaining 8 Tbsp [120 ml] olive oil, and the coriander.

When the pita pieces are cool, add them to the bowl and toss to incorporate. Season with salt and serve immediately. The fattoush can be made ahead, but you need to add the pita just before serving.

Lamb Chops

SERVES 4

4 lamb loin chops or rib chops

1 onion, thinly sliced

4 garlic cloves, smashed

4 Tbsp olive oil

2 bay leaves

1 Tbsp kosher salt

1 tsp ground allspice

½ tsp ground sumac

¼ tsp ground turmeric

¼ tsp ground cardamom

1 lemon, halved

1 fresh rosemary sprig, needles pulled from the stem and chopped

¼ cup [10 g] chopped fresh flat-leaf parsley

1 tsp chopped fresh mint

Put a towel under a large bowl and wear gloves (turmeric and sumac will stain your hands and countertops). Add the lamb, onion, garlic, 2 Tbsp of the olive oil, the bay leaves, salt, allspice, sumac, turmeric, and cardamom to the bowl. Squeeze the lemon juice into the bowl, then add the lemon halves to the bowl. Toss to fully coat the lamb. Marinate, uncovered, at room temperature for 1 hour or cover and refrigerate overnight or up to 3 days.

When ready to cook, heat a large skillet over medium-high heat. Add the remaining 2 Tbsp of olive oil, then add the lamb and sear, flipping, for 3 to 5 minutes on each side, or until lightly brown and slightly crispy, for medium-rare. For medium, turn the heat to medium and cook an additional 2 minutes on each side. Let rest at least 10 minutes, then sprinkle with the rosemary, parsley, and mint. Enjoy immediately or reheat in 400°F [200°C] oven for 3 to 5 minutes before serving. Store leftovers in an airtight container in the refrigerator for up to 3 days.

Lamb Kofta Kebabs

MAKES 10 TO 12 SKEWERS

2 Tbsp olive oil

1 onion, finely chopped

1 bell pepper, finely chopped

4 garlic cloves, minced

2 lbs [910 g] ground lamb

1 lb [455 g] ground beef

½ cup [30 g] panko

1 large egg

½ cup [20 g] chopped fresh flat-leaf parsley, plus more for serving

¼ cup [5 g] chopped fresh cilantro, plus more for serving

1 Tbsp kosher salt

2 tsp ground cumin

2 tsp ground coriander

1 tsp smoked paprika

Tiny pinch of ground cinnamon

8 to 10 turns freshly ground black pepper

1 lemon, cut into wedges

Wooden skewers, soaked in water for at least 10 minutes

Preheat the oven to 400°F [200°C]. Set a rack in a baking sheet or line the baking sheet with parchment paper.

In a medium sauté pan, heat the olive oil over medium heat. Add the onion, bell pepper, and garlic and cook for 3 minutes, or until the onion is slightly golden and somewhat translucent. Transfer to a medium bowl, then add the lamb, beef, panko, egg, parsley, cilantro, salt, cumin, coriander, paprika, cinnamon, and pepper and use your hands to mix until fully combined. Form the mixture into oblong meatballs, each roughly the size and shape of an egg. Thread one kofta or several on the soaked wooden skewers, then arrange the skewers on the prepared baking sheet and bake for 15 to 20 minutes, or until firm to the touch and cooked through for medium. Sprinkle with more parsley and cilantro and serve with the lemon wedges, Tzatziki (page 193), and Homemade Pita (page 195).

Cucumber Collins

MAKES 1 PITCHER (4 TO 6 DRINKS)

10 to 15 fresh mint leaves, plus more for serving

6 to 8 oz [180 to 240 ml] gin or vodka

4 to 6 oz [120 to 180 ml] simple syrup

Reserved liquid of 1 grated cucumber (from Tzatziki, page 193)

Juice of 2 limes

Three or four 12 oz [360 ml] cans seltzer

In a pitcher, muddle the mint leaves, then stir in the gin or vodka, simple syrup, reserved cucumber liquid, and lime juice. When ready to serve, add ice to glasses and fill halfway with the mint mixture. Top with the seltzer and stir. Garnish with more mint and enjoy.

PIZZA NIGHT

PART **IV**

POTLUCKS & SUPPER CLUBS

Everyone loves pizza. Everyone. Ever met someone who says they hate fresh bread loaded with cheese and other delicious accoutrements? Nope, probably not. I love hosting pizza night, and my guests love it even more. Have the dough ready, the toppings all set, and then let your guests roll the dough and garnish however they like. I've included the perfect recipes for the essentials, plus all sorts of topping suggestions for creating a pizza bar. When it comes to the basics— pesto, for example—I recommend making your own. And my red

sauce is a pure play of tart, bright notes you just can't get from a jar. If you want some additional variety, I've included a delicious veggie-heavy pizza with bold flavor, a pizza with brunch flair, and Tarte Flambée. You won't find these on the Domino's menu!

Suggested Potluck Sides and Dessert:

- Green salad
- Honey Piri-Piri Wings (page 161)
- If you aren't up for making dessert, pick up cannoli or tiramisu from your favorite Italian spot

The Essentials

Focaccia Crust

MAKES 2 OR 3 SMALL BAKING SHEET–SIZE PIZZAS

One ¼ oz [7 g] package active dry yeast

1 tsp granulated sugar

5½ cups [770 g] all-purpose flour, plus more as needed

¼ cup [60 ml] olive oil, plus 3 Tbsp for drizzling

1 tsp kosher salt

Toppings (recipes follow)

Brush a large bowl with olive oil.

In the bowl of a stand mixer fitted with the dough hook attachment, whisk together the yeast, sugar, and 1½ cups [360 ml] of warm water. Add the flour, ¼ cup [60 ml] of the olive oil, and the salt and mix on low speed to combine. Turn the mixer to medium-high speed and knead for 5 to 8 minutes, or until the dough is smooth, slightly sticky, and is pulling away from the sides and forming a loose ball around the hook. If the dough is not pulling away from the sides of the bowl, add ¼ cup [35 g] more flour and continue mixing. Loosely cover the dough with plastic wrap or a thin towel, put it in the prepared bowl, and let rest at room temperature for 1 hour, or until doubled in size. Alternatively, let the dough rest overnight in the refrigerator; the next day, let the dough sit at room temperature for 1 to 2 hours before using.

When ready to make pizza, preheat the oven as high as it will go, 450 to 500°F [230 to 260°C].

On a floured work surface, use a rolling pin to roll out the dough to fit a baking sheet or pizza stone. Drizzle with the remaining 3 Tbsp of olive oil and then add the desired toppings and bake for about 15 minutes, or until the cheese is bubbling and the sides of the crust are golden all over and speckled with toasted brown spots. Let the pizza cool for at least 10 minutes before slicing and serving.

Pesto

MAKES ABOUT 2 CUPS [520 G]

2 cups [24 g] fresh basil leaves or arugula

2 garlic cloves, peeled

2 Tbsp pine nuts (or 4 to 6 walnuts or almonds)

½ cup [120 ml] extra-virgin olive oil

Zest and juice of 1 lemon

½ cup [15 g] grated Parmesan cheese

8 to 10 turns freshly ground black pepper

Pinch of red pepper flakes (optional)

Kosher salt

In a food processor, combine the basil or arugula, garlic, and pine nuts and process until minced. With the processor running, gradually add the olive oil in a very fine, slow drizzle and process until mostly smooth. Add the lemon zest and juice, Parmesan, black pepper, and red pepper flakes and pulse until just combined. Season with salt. Use immediately or refrigerate in an airtight container for up to 2 weeks.

Red Sauce

MAKES 4 TO 6 CUPS [880 G TO 1.3 KG]

3 Tbsp olive oil

2 cups [300 g] cherry tomatoes or chopped ripe tomatoes

Kosher salt

1 onion, chopped

6 garlic cloves, minced

One 32 oz [910 g] can crushed tomatoes

8 to 10 turns freshly ground black pepper

6 to 10 red pepper flakes

In a large sauté pan, heat the olive oil over high heat. Add the fresh tomatoes and 1 Tbsp of salt and cook for 10 to 15 minutes, or until they burst and blister. Turn the heat to low, then add the onion and garlic and cook for 5 to 8 minutes, or until they have sweated and are translucent. Add the canned tomatoes, black pepper, and red pepper flakes. Season with salt. Simmer on low heat for 20 minutes or up to 1 hour. Serve immediately or let cool and refrigerate in an airtight container for up to 2 weeks or freeze for up to 3 months.

Pizza Toppings Bar

Proteins & Dairy

Bacon, barbecue chicken, duck confit, fresh mozzarella, goat cheese, grated Gruyère, grated Parmesan cheese, ham, ricotta, sausage, shredded mozzarella, shrimp, smoked salmon

Fruits & Veggies

Arugula, caramelized onions, chopped kale, figs, green onions, grilled and/or raw stone fruit (such as peaches), halved cherry tomatoes, roasted or caramelized fennel, sautéed mushrooms, sliced peppers, sliced tomatoes, spinach, zucchini noodles

Condiments

Balsamic vinegar, Calabrian chiles, chili crunch, herb oils, honey, marinated artichokes, olive tapenade, pine nuts, red pepper flakes, truffle oil, walnuts

MY FAVORITE COMBOS

Fresh pear or fig, caramelized onion, ricotta, and honey

Cherry tomatoes and pesto, finished with arugula and red pepper flakes

Mushrooms, kale, mozzarella, and grated Parmesan cheese, finished with basil and olive oil

Fennel, caramelized onions, green olives, and goat cheese

Crème fraîche, bacon, ham, soppressata, and green onions, finished with arugula, Calabrian chiles, and olive oil

Mozzarella and sliced tomato, finished with prosciutto, arugula, and olive oil

Goat cheese, sautéed mushrooms, shaved truffles, and truffle oil

Spicy Summer Squash Pizza

SERVES 4 TO 6

Focaccia Crust (page 204)

4 cups [320 g] zucchini noodles

2 Tbsp kosher salt

1 cup [100 g] chopped green onions, green and white parts

4 cups [460 g] grated Gruyère cheese

2 cups [120 g] panko

1 cup [30 g] finely grated Parmesan cheese

2 Tbsp chili crunch

Prepare the focaccia crust as directed until it's ready for toppings.

In a colander, toss the zucchini noodles with the salt. Let stand for 15 to 30 minutes to allow the liquid to release. Gently press and squeeze the noodles to remove as much liquid as possible, then transfer to a medium bowl; discard the liquid. Add the green onions and Gruyère to the noodles and toss to combine, then place on top of the prepared dough.

In a medium bowl, toss together the panko, Parmesan, and chili crunch. Sprinkle this over the pizza and bake as directed for the focaccia crust.

Everything Bagel Pizza

SERVES 4 TO 6

Focaccia Crust (page 204)

8 oz [230 g] Boursin garlic and herb spread

2 lbs [910 g] thinly sliced smoked salmon

1 lemon, halved and very thinly sliced

2 cups [60 g] arugula

2 Tbsp capers, drained

2 Tbsp everything bagel seasoning

1 bunch fresh dill

2 Tbsp extra-virgin olive oil

Prepare the focaccia crust as directed, and bake without the toppings. Let the crust cool to room temperature, then spread the Boursin over the entire surface. Add a layer of sliced salmon, followed by the lemon slices. Sprinkle with the arugula, capers, everything bagel seasoning, and dill. Drizzle with the olive oil and enjoy immediately.

Tarte Flambée

SERVES 4 TO 6

Focaccia Crust (page 204)

1 cup [200 g] fromage blanc

½ cup [120 g] crème fraîche

Zest of 1 lemon

¼ tsp ground white pepper

Pinch of freshly ground nutmeg

Kosher salt

4 shallots, very thinly sliced, preferably on a mandoline

4 oz [115 g] thick bacon, cut into lardons
(the lardons cut is crucial)

Prepare the focaccia crust up until the point that it is ready to be rolled out.

Preheat the oven as high as it will go, 450 to 500°F [230 to 260°C].

On a floured work surface, use a rolling pin to roll out the focaccia dough into one or two large, thin ovals. (Whether you make one or two depends on the size of your baking sheet; all that matters is that this is a thin crust flatbread.) Place the rolled dough on a baking sheet or pizza stone, then drizzle with 3 Tbsp of olive oil per the focaccia crust recipe.

In a medium bowl, whisk together the fromage blanc, crème fraîche, lemon zest, white pepper, and nutmeg. Season with salt, then spread this mixture on the pizza dough, leaving about 1 in [2.5 cm] around the edges. Scatter with the shallots, followed by the bacon. Bake for 10 to 15 minutes, or until the dough has puffed up, the crust is golden, and the bacon is crisp. Serve immediately.

Tiramisu

SERVES 6 TO 8

4 large egg yolks

½ cup [100 g] granulated sugar

1 cup [240 ml] heavy cream

1 cup [240 g] mascarpone

2 cups [480 ml] brewed espresso or strong coffee, chilled

2 Tbsp rum or Cognac

1 Tbsp amaretto liqueur

2 Tbsp unsweetened cocoa powder

25 to 30 ladyfingers

1 tsp flaky salt

2 oz [55 g] bittersweet chocolate

In the bowl of a stand mixer fitted with the whisk attachment, combine the egg yolks and ¼ cup [50 g] of the sugar and whip on high speed for about 10 minutes, or until very pale yellow and tripled in volume. Transfer the mixture to a large bowl.

Wipe out the stand mixer bowl and clean the whisk. Add the heavy cream and the remaining ¼ cup [50 g] of sugar and whip on high speed until soft peaks form. Add the mascarpone and continue whipping on high speed until semi-stiff peaks form. Add the mascarpone mixture to the egg yolk mixture and fold until combined.   cont.

In a 9 by 12 in [23 by 30.5 cm] casserole dish, combine the espresso or coffee with the rum or Cognac and amaretto liqueur. Set aside.

Sift 1 Tbsp of the cocoa powder on the bottom of an 8 by 8 in [20 by 20 cm] dish or a 9 in [23 cm] round cake pan.

Working quickly, dip half of the ladyfingers into the espresso mixture—they are porous and will fall apart if left in the liquid too long. Arrange the dipped ladyfingers in a single layer on the bottom of the cocoa-dusted pan, cutting them as needed to fill the bottom of the pan. Spread half of the mascarpone mixture in an even layer over the ladyfingers. Quickly dip the remaining ladyfingers and arrange them in a single layer on top of the mascarpone layer. Add a second mascarpone layer. Dust the top layer of mascarpone with the remaining 1 Tbsp of cocoa powder, then sprinkle with salt and use a Microplane to grate the chocolate over the top. Cover with plastic wrap and refrigerate for at least 2 hours and preferably overnight. Tiramisu can be made ahead, wrapped in plastic wrap, and refrigerated for up to 3 days.

PART

V

SOUTHERN GET-TOGETHERS

Formal Affairs & Slow Food Socials

This chapter is about two types of planned dinners. First are the more formal affairs, the meals that you sit down for, at a table, maybe even with place cards. Nice china, cloth napkins, and stemware are all in play here. These might be business dinners or when you host new neighbors or future in-laws. You get the drift. These are not the times for pulling out new recipes. You make what you make best, and you execute it flawlessly. The second type of gathering is the more casual labor of love that you plan for the ones you love. These slow food weekend meals are for your own family or close friends and are opportunities to experiment with flavors and try new pairings.

    I'm a believer in mastering a recipe or technique and then letting your creativity flow. There is hardly

an occasion when Roast Chicken (page 222) or Fish en Papillote (page 241) isn't a delicious crowd-pleaser. They are the queens of classic French cooking and provide a perfect jumping off point for so many delicious variations. I've also included recipes for Paella (page 248) and Boeuf Bourguignon (page 257), which are both super flavorful, can be made for a full table, and, once they are mastered, are relatively easy. I encourage you to repeat a few of the recipes in this section in no-pressure situations so that when you have an event you'd like to celebrate, or new neighbors you'd like to invite over, you're ready with your mastered meal!

I'm also a believer in making time for the things and the ones you love. At our wedding, "A Sunday Kind of Love" by Etta James was our first dance. If only we knew then how the lyrics of that song would hold true for our lives. Sunday is the only day my restaurant is closed, and my husband, Deavours, rarely takes work calls. It's our one true day of rest. Often, we work in the yard, our favorite therapy. And just as often I choose to cook a good-for-your-soul, hug-your-heart kind of meal, another form of therapy. Sometimes we invite people over at the end of our day well spent, and sometimes we choose to spend a night at home as a family enjoying a really good meal together. Either way, these slow food Sundays are restorative and nourishing.

ROAST CHICKEN DINNER

PART

V

FORMAL AFFAIRS & SLOW FOOD SOCIALS

My answer is always roast chicken. Dinner that needs to impress? Roast chicken. Simple, satisfying weeknight meal? Roast chicken. Don't know what to cook for xyz? Roast chicken. Y'all, I mean it. A whole bird with perfectly golden, crispy skin is a sight to behold. It's not flashy, but it conveys an air of confidence in the kitchen. And when done well, it is the most wholesome and delicious of all foods. You'll be hard-pressed to find an occasion when roast chicken isn't welcome, and bonus, you'll never run out of variations for this foolproof dish. I've included some tried-and-true takes on my classic French poulet, as well as recommended sides. Lastly, don't sleep on roasting two birds—you'll want the leftovers.

Roast Chicken, Five Ways

SERVES 4 TO 6

No. One

One 3 to 5 lb [1.4 to 2.3 kg] chicken

½ cup [120 ml] olive oil

2 Tbsp kosher salt

1 head garlic

2 fresh rosemary sprigs

3 Tbsp dried lavender or 2 fresh thyme sprigs

1 lemon, halved

Twine, for trussing

Pat down the chicken with paper towels and place it on a rack set inside a baking sheet. Refrigerate the chicken, uncovered, overnight or up to 2 days. If you're in a time crunch, instead of refrigerating the chicken, whip out a blow-dryer and blow on the chicken skin for about 5 minutes. This dries out the skin, which makes the meat hold moisture and the skin crisp like a potato chip.

When ready to roast the chicken, preheat the oven to 425°F [220°C].

Rub the chicken with the olive oil and salt. Smash the garlic cloves with the back of a knife to open them up, then put the cloves, along with the rosemary and lavender or thyme, inside the chicken cavity. Squeeze the lemon over the chicken, then put the lemon halves inside the cavity. Use twine to truss the chicken, then roast in the middle of the oven for 1 hour, or until the internal temperature reaches 165°F [74°C]. Turn the oven off but leave the chicken to rest in the oven for 20 minutes. Remove the chicken from the oven and let it rest at room temperature for another 20 minutes. Carve and enjoy the best roast chicken you've ever had.   cont.

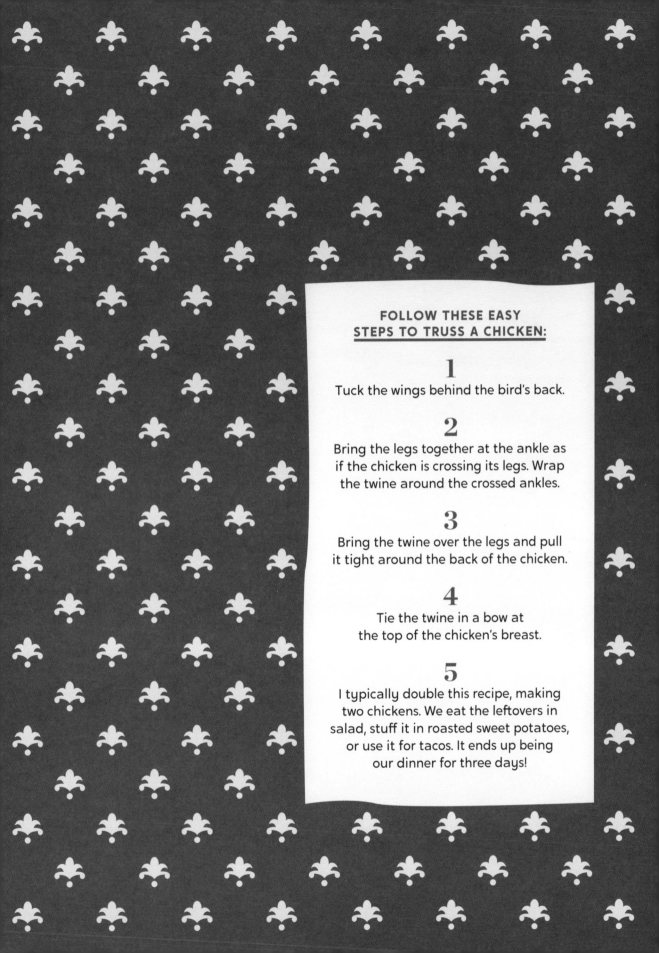

**FOLLOW THESE EASY
STEPS TO TRUSS A CHICKEN:**

1

Tuck the wings behind the bird's back.

2

Bring the legs together at the ankle as
if the chicken is crossing its legs. Wrap
the twine around the crossed ankles.

3

Bring the twine over the legs and pull
it tight around the back of the chicken.

4

Tie the twine in a bow at
the top of the chicken's breast.

5

I typically double this recipe, making
two chickens. We eat the leftovers in
salad, stuff it in roasted sweet potatoes,
or use it for tacos. It ends up being
our dinner for three days!

No. Two
Fennel and Citrus Roast Chicken

SERVES 4 TO 6

1 fennel bulb, thinly sliced

4 sweet potatoes, halved lengthwise

One 3 to 5 lb [1.4 to 2.3 kg] chicken

½ cup [120 ml] olive oil

2 Tbsp kosher salt

3 Tbsp smoked paprika

3 Tbsp fennel seeds

Pinch of cayenne pepper

1 orange, halved

Preheat the oven to 425°F [220°C].

Spread the fennel in a single layer in a 14 or 16 in [35.5 to 40.5 cm] roasting pan. Put the sweet potatoes, cut-side down, on top to protect the fennel from burning. Prepare the chicken as directed (see page 222), rubbing with the olive oil and salt, then sprinkling with the paprika, fennel, and cayenne. Squeeze the orange all over the chicken, then place the chicken directly on top of the sweet potatoes and roast as directed. Serve with the Chickpea Salad (page 245).

No. Three
Piri-Piri Roast Chicken

SERVES 4 TO 6

1 bunch fresh cilantro

6 garlic cloves, peeled

6 to 8 slices peeled fresh ginger

1 shallot, chopped

½ cup piri-piri sauce [120 ml] plus 3 Tbsp

½ cup olive oil [120 ml] plus 2 Tbsp

2 lemons, halved

One 3 to 5 lb [1.4 to 2.3 kg] chicken

2 Tbsp kosher salt

Separate the cilantro stems and leaves and chop each separately. Put the stems in a large bowl; reserve the leaves for the glaze.

Smash 3 garlic cloves with the back of a knife and add them to the bowl with the cilantro stems. Add the ginger, shallot, ½ cup [120 ml] of piri-piri sauce, ½ cup [120 ml] of olive oil, and the juice from one lemon. Add the chicken to the bowl, turn to coat, cover, and refrigerate overnight.

When ready to roast the chicken, preheat the oven to 425°F [220°C] and roast the chicken as directed (see page 222).

Meanwhile, make the glaze: Mince the remaining 3 garlic cloves and put them in a small pot. Add the reserved chopped cilantro leaves, the remaining 3 Tbsp of piri-piri sauce, the remaining 2 Tbsp of olive oil, and the juice from the remaining lemon. Bring to a simmer and cook for about 5 minutes, or until the liquid thickens. Pour this glaze over the chicken. Serve with a simple green salad and roasted new potatoes.

No. Four
Peruvian Roast Chicken

SERVES 4 TO 6

1 Tbsp garlic powder

1 Tbsp onion powder

1 Tbsp ground cumin

1 Tbsp paprika

1 Tbsp dried basil

1 Tbsp ground coriander

1 tsp kosher salt

1 tsp freshly ground black pepper

1 tsp dried oregano

½ tsp ground fennel

⅛ tsp ground cinnamon

⅛ tsp ground nutmeg

One 3 to 5 lb [1.4 to 2.3 kg] chicken

2 lemons, halved

Preheat the oven to 425°F [220°C].

In a small bowl, combine the garlic powder, onion powder, cumin, paprika, basil, coriander, salt, pepper, oregano, fennel, cinnamon, and nutmeg. Rub the mixture all over the chicken and inside the cavity. Squeeze the lemons over the chicken and put the lemon halves inside the cavity. Roast the chicken as directed (see page 222). Serve with quinoa and the Peruvian Solterito Salad (page 226).

No. Five
Middle Eastern–Style Roast Chicken

SERVES 4 TO 6

8 to 10 large carrots, peeled

One 3 to 5 lb [1.4 to 2.3 kg] chicken

½ cup [170 g] honey

1 cup [260 g] harissa paste

2 Tbsp olive oil

¼ cup [40 g] coriander seeds

2 Tbsp kosher salt

1 Tbsp paprika

1 tsp ground fenugreek

1 tsp ground turmeric

1 tsp ground ginger

½ tsp ground cumin

Pinch of ground cinnamon

Pinch of ground allspice

Preheat the oven to 425°F [220°C].

Put the carrots in a 14 or 16 in [35.5 to 40.5 cm] roasting pan. Set a rack over the carrots, then place the chicken on the rack.

In a medium bowl, combine the honey and 2 Tbsp of hot water and whisk to dissolve the honey. Whisk in the harissa and olive oil. Drizzle all over the bird, rubbing it in and letting some drip down onto the carrots.

In a small bowl, combine the coriander, salt, paprika, fenugreek, turmeric, ginger, cumin, cinnamon, and allspice. Rub all over the chicken and inside the cavity. Roast the chicken as directed (see page 222) but baste the carrots in the chicken fat every 15 to 20 minutes. If the carrots start to dry out, add 1 cup [240 ml] water or chicken stock. Serve with Fattoush (page 197).

Peruvian Solterito Salad

SERVES 4 TO 6

2 cups [280 g] fresh or frozen lima beans or edamame

2 cups [280 g] fresh or frozen corn kernels

1 cup [150 g] cherry tomatoes, halved

1 small red onion, finely diced

1 jalapeño, seeded and minced

¼ cup [35 g] pitted and chopped Kalamata olives

1 cup [120 g] crumbled feta

¼ cup [10 g] chopped fresh parsley

¼ cup [10 g] chopped fresh cilantro

4 to 6 Tbsp [60 to 90 ml] olive oil

Juice of 1 lemon

Kosher salt

Freshly ground black pepper

If using frozen lima beans or edamame or frozen corn, thaw before using.

In a medium bowl, combine the lima beans or edamame, corn, tomatoes, red onion, jalapeño, and olives. Add the feta, parsley, cilantro, olive oil, and lemon juice and toss to combine. Season with salt and pepper. Serve immediately or refrigerate in an airtight container for up to 3 days.

Jollof Rice

SERVES 4 TO 6

Obe Ata (see Note)

1 lb [455 g] fresh tomatoes or one 14 oz [400 g] can whole peeled tomatoes with their juices

2 bell peppers, roughly chopped

1 red onion, roughly chopped

6 garlic cloves, peeled

One 1 in [2.5 cm] piece fresh ginger, peeled and chopped

1 habanero or Scotch bonnet chile

2 Tbsp canola or other neutral oil

Rice

¼ cup [60 ml] canola or other neutral oil

¼ cup [55 g] unsalted butter

2 red onions, thinly sliced

4 garlic cloves, thinly sliced

2 Tbsp tomato paste

1 tsp ground turmeric

½ tsp smoked paprika

3 cups [600 g] basmati or jasmine rice

3 fresh thyme sprigs

2 bay leaves

2 Tbsp salt

8 to 10 turns freshly ground black pepper

2 cups [475 ml] chicken stock

½ cup [20 g] chopped fresh flat-leaf parsley

½ cup [50 g] chopped green onions, green and white parts

To make the obe ata: In a food processor or blender, combine the tomatoes, bell peppers, red onion, garlic, ginger, and habanero or Scotch bonnet chile and process on high speed until mostly smooth.

In a medium saucepan, warm the canola oil over high heat. Add the pepper purée, bring to a simmer, and cook for 20 minutes, or until reduced by one-third; you should have about 2 cups [475 ml]. Remove from the heat.   cont.

To make the rice: Preheat the oven to 350°F [180°C].

In a large Dutch oven, heat the canola oil and butter over medium-low heat. Add the red onions and garlic and cook, stirring frequently, for about 5 minutes, or until slightly translucent. Add the tomato paste, turmeric, and paprika. Stir in the obe ata sauce and bring to a simmer over medium heat. Stir in the rice, thyme, bay leaves, salt, and pepper, then stir in the chicken stock, cover, and transfer the pot to the oven. Bake for 25 to 35 minutes, or until the rice is just tender. Remove the pot from the oven and let stand, covered, for 15 minutes—this needs to be exact, so set a timer. Uncover the pot, fluff the rice with a fork, and discard the thyme and bay leaves. Sprinkle with the parsley and green onions and serve warm.

NOTE

Obe ata, which translates to "fried pepper stew" or just "pepper stew," is a tomato-based sauce that is a staple in Nigerian cuisine. It's eaten at breakfast with eggs as well as for lunch and dinner—a versatile recipe indeed. I often quadruple the obe ata recipe and then freeze it in 2 cup [475 ml] portions for easy, quick weeknight meals.

STAYCATION SHRIMP SOIREE

PART

V

FORMAL AFFAIRS & SLOW FOOD SOCIALS

When I was first married, my new husband could not understand why I had so many plates, glasses, and silverware. "Why do we need twelve wine glasses in six colors? Why do you keep buying plates when we have plenty?" The answer was simple. If I'm going to live in a small town, with a limited restaurant scene, little variety, and not a lot of ambiance, then I'm going to create the damn things myself. Cooking new foods and creating a pleasing atmosphere, while doting on and enjoying my friends, became my new passion.

This menu is one of my favorites for entertaining at home. I first had these plump, perfect shrimp in New Orleans, and this menu transports me to that magical, musical city known as the Big Easy. I especially love that this dish is hands on, which means cell phones are left untouched, as everyone peels the shrimp, dips hunks of bread in the liquid gold that is the broth, and just enjoys being in the moment. Wrap this meal up with the fancy flair of Bananas Foster, blues cooing in the background, twinkling lights above, and you just may believe you're sitting on Frenchmen Street.

NOLA Barbecue Shrimp

SERVES 4 TO 6

2 cups [452 g] unsalted butter

¼ cup [60 ml] Worcestershire sauce

2 Tbsp soy sauce

1 Tbsp fish sauce

6 to 8 garlic cloves, minced

2 celery stalks, finely chopped

2 shallots or leeks, finely chopped

3 bay leaves

1 Tbsp Cajun seasoning

1 Tbsp paprika

6 to 8 dashes Tabasco or Crystal hot sauce

2 lemons

2 to 3 lbs [910 g to 1.4 kg] large shrimp, head and shells on

Kosher salt

Freshly ground black pepper

1 bunch fresh flat-leaf parsley, leaves chopped

1 bunch green onions, green and white parts, chopped

1 to 2 loaves crusty French bread, cut into big hunks

In a large Dutch oven or wok, combine the butter, Worcestershire sauce, soy sauce, fish sauce, garlic, celery, shallots or leeks, bay leaves, Cajun seasoning, paprika, and hot sauce. Cut 1 of the lemons into slices and add to the pot. Bring to a boil over high heat, then lower the heat to a simmer and cook for 10 minutes, until fragrant. Add the shrimp, cover, and cook, stirring occasionally, for about 15 minutes, or until the shrimp just turn pink. Cut the remaining lemon in half and squeeze over the pot. Stir to incorporate, then season with salt and pepper. Garnish with the parsley and green onions. Serve hot with the bread to mop up the sauce and Whole Artichokes (page 234) on the side.

Whole Artichokes

SERVES 4 TO 6

4 artichokes, leaves and stems trimmed

1 lemon, halved

1 onion, chopped

1 celery stalk, chopped

4 garlic cloves, peeled

2 Tbsp Cajun seasoning

In a large stockpot with a lid, combine the artichokes, lemon, onion, celery, garlic, Cajun seasoning, and enough water to completely submerge the artichokes. Cover and bring to a rolling boil over high heat. Continue boiling for 30 to 45 minutes, or until the artichoke leaves easily pull away. Drain the artichokes and serve simply alongside drawn butter or, in this case, with the NOLA Barbecue Shrimp (page 233), using the buttery shrimp sauce for the artichokes.

> **NOTE**
>
> You can cook the artichokes ahead and store them in an airtight container in the refrigerator for up to 3 days. Reheat the artichokes in the microwave for a few minutes when you're ready to enjoy them.

Bananas Foster

SERVES 8

1 cup [226 g] unsalted butter

2 cups [400 g] packed dark brown sugar

4 bananas, halved lengthwise

1 cup [240 ml] dark rum

¼ cup [60 ml] heavy cream

Pinch of kosher salt

1 cup [120 g] chopped pecans

Vanilla ice cream, for serving

In a medium or large sauté pan, melt the butter and brown sugar over low heat. Turn the heat to medium, then add the bananas, cut-side down, and sauté, turning the bananas once, for 2 minutes, or until lightly browned. Remove the pan from the heat and add the rum, then put the pan over high heat to flambé the bananas, gently swirling the liquid and keeping your face away from the pan, for 2 to 3 minutes, or until the fire goes out. Turn off the heat, then tilt the pan and push the bananas to one side. Add the heavy cream and salt to the sauce, whisking until fully combined, then add the pecans, stirring to coat them in the sauce.

Scoop vanilla ice cream into bowls, then place a banana half in each bowl, drizzle with sauce, and serve.

NOTE

Typically, there is no heavy cream in this sauce, but it's my little catering trick. The cream stabilizes the caramel, so you can make it ahead and let it stand at room temperature until you're ready to serve it. The pecans, also not traditional, add the perfect crunch to round out this dessert.

WORLD'S BEST FISH (IN A BAG!) DINNER

Fish en papillote sounds so fancy, so romantic, so very French, doesn't it? But I have a little secret for y'all: It's literally just fish in a paper bag. Leave it to the French to make something so simple sound so dazzling. This was one of the first recipes I mastered in culinary school, so it holds a nostalgic and loving place in my heart. What's more, it's mess-free, smell-free, and can be cooked perfectly every single time in just twenty minutes. Lastly, fish en papillote is quite possibly the easiest protein to cook for a large crowd. Simply double, triple, or quadruple the recipe and fill your oven with balloons of the most delicately cooked and herbaceous fish you've ever tasted. Top the classic recipe with Corn Maque Choux and Tarragon Cream Sauce and serve alongside Chickpea Salad or take one of the variations on the fish recipe out for a spin.

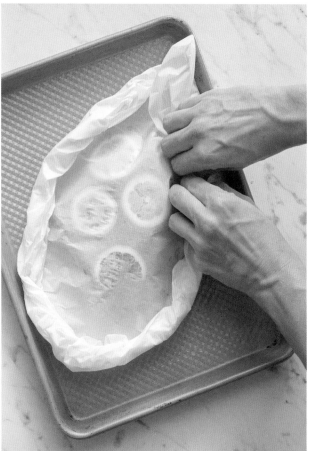

Fish en Papillote, Six Ways

SERVES 4 TO 6

No. One

2 bay leaves

1 onion, thinly sliced

3 garlic cloves, peeled

1 lemon, thinly sliced

One 2 to 3 lb [910 g to 1.4 kg] side of fish
or four 6 to 8 oz [170 to 230 g] fillets (see Note)

1 Tbsp olive oil

1 Tbsp kosher salt

8 to 10 turns freshly ground black pepper

NOTE

Use for fish en papillote:
Bass
Catfish
Cod
Flounder
Grouper
Haddock
Halibut
Salmon
Snapper

Preheat the oven to 425°F [220°C]. Tear two pieces of parchment paper or aluminum foil, each about the size of a baking sheet, and place one on a baking sheet.

Layer the bay leaves, onion, garlic, and lemon on the parchment or foil on the baking sheet. Arrange the fish on top, then drizzle with the olive oil and sprinkle with the salt and pepper. Place the other sheet of parchment or foil over the fish and crimp the sides all the way around, sealing the two pieces of parchment or foil together. Bake for 15 to 20 minutes, or until the fish is cooked through and flakes easily with a fork. Remove the fish from the paper or foil, plate, then top with Tarragon Cream Sauce (page 245) and Corn Maque Choux (page 244). Note that for variations without sauce or toppings, you can simply open the paper or foil, garnish, and serve the fish still in its wrapping.   cont.

No. Two
Mediterranean Fish en Papillote

SERVES 4 TO 6

¼ cup [35 g] pitted and sliced Kalamata or green olives

1 Tbsp capers, drained

½ cup [75 g] cherry tomatoes

½ cup [100 g] jarred marinated whole artichoke hearts

One 2 to 3 lb [910 g to 1.4 kg] side of fish or four 6 to 8 oz [170 to 230 g] fillets

5 fresh basil leaves, torn, for serving

1 lemon, halved, for serving

Preheat the oven to 425°F [220°C] and prepare the Fish en Papillote (see page 241) as directed, layering the olives, capers, tomatoes, and artichoke hearts on the parchment paper or aluminum foil and arranging the fish on top before sealing the parchment or foil. Bake as directed. Sprinkle with the basil and drizzle with a squeeze of lemon. Serve with Tzatziki Fusilli Salad (page 72) and spinach sautéed in butter or olive oil.

No. Three
Thai Fish en Papillote

SERVES 4 TO 6

3 Tbsp fish sauce

3 Tbsp chili crunch

2 Tbsp tamarind paste

2 Tbsp light brown sugar

1 bunch fresh cilantro

One 2 to 3 lb [910 g to 1.4 kg] side of fish or four 6 to 8 oz [170 to 230 g] fillets

¼ cup [50 g] chopped green onions, green and white parts

2 Tbsp chopped peanuts

Juice of 1 lime

Preheat the oven to 425°F [220°C]. Tear two pieces of parchment paper or aluminum foil, each about the size of a baking sheet, and place one on a baking sheet.

In a small bowl, whisk together the fish sauce, 2 Tbsp of the chili crunch, the tamarind paste, and the brown sugar.

Separate the cilantro leaves and stems. Chop the leaves and set them aside. Place the cilantro stems on the parchment or foil on the baking sheet, then pour the fish sauce mixture over them and arrange the fish on top. Bake the Fish en Papillote (see page 241) as directed.

While the fish is baking, in a medium bowl, combine the reserved cilantro leaves with the remaining 1 Tbsp of chili crunch, the green onions, peanuts, and lime juice.

Arrange the cilantro salad on top of the fish and serve with white rice and sautéed greens, such as bok choy, broccolini, spinach, or kale.

No. Four
Cantonese Fish en Papillote

SERVES 4 TO 6

1 cup [100 g] finely chopped green onions, white and green parts

¼ cup [25 g] julienned peeled fresh ginger

2 Tbsp soy sauce

Pinch of ground white pepper

One 2 to 3 lb [910 g to 1.4 kg] side of fish or four 6 to 8 oz [170 to 230 g] fillets

Preheat the oven to 425°F [220°C] and prepare the Fish en Papillote (see page 241) as directed, layering the green onions, ginger, soy sauce, and white pepper on the parchment paper or aluminum foil and arranging the fish on top before sealing the parchment or foil. Bake as directed. Serve with white rice.

No. Five
Mexican Fish en Papillote

SERVES 4 TO 6

1 Tbsp chopped canned chipotle chiles in adobo

¼ cup [65 g] Salsa Verde (page 186)

One 2 to 3 lb [910 g to 1.4 kg] side of fish or four 6 to 8 oz [170 to 230 g] fillets

1 bunch fresh cilantro, leaves chopped

Juice of 1 lime

Preheat the oven to 425°F [220°C] and prepare the Fish en Papillote (see page 241) as directed, layering the chipotle chiles and Salsa Verde on the parchment paper or aluminum foil and arranging the fish on top before sealing the parchment or foil. Bake as directed.

Sprinkle with the cilantro, drizzle with the lime juice, and serve with Spanish or yellow rice and black or refried beans or Black Beans and Rice (page 148).

No. Six
Basque Fish en Papillote

SERVES 4 TO 6

1 bell pepper, thinly sliced

1 tomato, thinly sliced

One 2 to 3 lb [910 g to 1.4 kg] side of fish or four 6 to 8 oz [170 to 230 g] fillets

1 tsp smoked paprika

Pinch of Espelette pepper or cayenne pepper

Pinch of saffron threads

1 bunch fresh flat-leaf parsley, leaves chopped

Preheat the oven to 425°F [220°C] and prepare the Fish en Papillote (see page 241) as directed, layering the bell pepper and tomato on the parchment paper or aluminum foil and arranging the fish on top. Sprinkle with the paprika, Espelette pepper or cayenne, and saffron before sealing the parchment or foil. Bake as directed. Sprinkle with the chopped parsley and serve with Arugula and Parmesan Salad (page 74), and/or Zucchini Gratin (page 132).

Corn Maque Choux

SERVES 4

8 oz [230 g] bacon, diced

3 Tbsp unsalted butter

8 ears fresh white corn, shucked, or 4 cups [560 g] frozen corn kernels

1 large onion, diced

1 bell pepper, diced

1 celery stalk, diced

4 garlic cloves, minced

¼ cup [60 ml] heavy cream

½ tsp Old Bay Seasoning

6 to 8 dashes Tabasco or Crystal hot sauce

1 lemon, halved

Kosher salt

½ cup [50 g] chopped green onions, green and white parts

¼ cup [10 g] chopped fresh flat-leaf parsley

In a medium to large cast-iron skillet or nonstick pan, cook the bacon over low heat for 10 to 15 minutes, or until the fat is completely rendered. Remove from the heat and, using a slotted spoon, transfer the bacon to a paper towel–lined plate.

Add the butter to the bacon fat in the pan. Place the pan over low heat and melt the butter. Turn the heat to medium, add the corn, and cook for 8 to 10 minutes to release the water and caramelize the corn until golden in color. Add the onion, bell pepper, celery, and garlic and cook, stirring and scraping the bottom of the pan, for 5 minutes, or until golden. Turn the heat to low, add the heavy cream, Old Bay, and hot sauce and cook for 5 minutes, or until thickened. Squeeze the lemon over the corn and season with salt. Sprinkle with the green onions, parsley, and bacon bits and serve hot atop the Fish en Papillote (page 241).

Tarragon Cream Sauce

MAKES ½ CUP [120 ML]

3 Tbsp unsalted butter

1 Tbsp all-purpose flour

1 cup [240 ml] dry white wine

¼ tsp Old Bay Seasoning

½ cup [120 ml] heavy cream

1 tsp fresh or dried tarragon

Kosher salt

Freshly ground black pepper

In a medium nonstick frying pan, melt 2 Tbsp of the butter over medium-low heat. Whisk in the flour until combined, then add the white wine and Old Bay and cook for about 2 minutes, or until the mixture begins to thicken and just coats the back of a spoon but still drips. Add the heavy cream and tarragon and season with salt and pepper. Whisk in the remaining 1 Tbsp of butter and serve over the fish. This can be made ahead and stored in an airtight container in the refrigerator for up to 3 days. Warm in a pan over medium-low heat.

Chickpea Salad

SERVES 4 TO 6

Two 15 oz [425 g] cans chickpeas, drained and rinsed

1 cup [120 g] crumbled feta

½ cup [70 g] pitted Castelvetrano or green olives

½ cup [20 g] chopped fresh flat-leaf parsley

¼ cup [60 ml] olive oil

Juice of 1 lemon

10 turns freshly ground black pepper

Kosher salt

In a serving bowl, combine the chickpeas, feta, olives, and parsley. Add the olive oil, lemon juice, and pepper. Season with salt, toss to combine, and serve immediately. The chickpea salad can be made ahead and stored in an airtight container in the refrigerator for up to 2 days.

PAELLA NIGHT

PART

V

FORMAL AFFAIRS & SLOW FOOD SOCIALS

I cook paella when I want to impress, but the secret is that it is really freaking easy, y'all. It's rice, studded with threads of saffron and an ample amount of seafood. Pair it with slices of tart and crunchy Pan con Tomate and refreshing Spanish Red Sangria then finish the evening with Flan de Leche and you'll transport your guests to the Spanish coast.

Paella

SERVES 6 TO 8

1 lb [455 g] shell-on shrimp

5 cups [1.2 L] chicken stock

2 bay leaves

1 bunch fresh parsley

4 green onions

¼ cup [60 ml] olive oil

8 oz [230 g] dried or fresh chorizo, chopped

1 red bell pepper, chopped

1 onion, chopped

4 garlic cloves, minced

2 Tbsp kosher salt

One 14 oz [400 g] can diced tomatoes with their juices

1 cup [240 ml] dry white wine

2 cups [400 g] short-grain rice

1 Tbsp saffron threads

½ tsp smoked paprika

1 cup [135 g] frozen peas, thawed

1 lb [455 g] mussels, clams, scallops, lobster, or crab

1 lb [455 g] white fish (see Note)

2 lemons, cut into wedges

Peel the shrimp and reserve the shells; set the shrimp aside.

In a medium stockpot or Dutch oven over medium heat, toast the shrimp shells, stirring, for about 2 minutes. Add the chicken stock and bay leaves. Separate the parsley stems and leaves, reserving the leaves for garnish, then add the stems to the stock. Separate the bulbs and stalks of the green onions, reserving the stalks for garnish, then add the bulbs to the stock. Bring the stock to a boil, then lower the heat to a simmer and cook for at least 30 minutes while you prepare the sofrito. Strain the stock before using, keeping it hot to add to the paella.

NOTE

Use in paella:
Obia
Cod
Grouper
Redfish
Snapper

I always recommend selecting whatever is the freshest and most local.

In a large paella pan or large, deep sauté pan, warm the olive oil over medium-low heat. Add the chorizo, bell pepper, onion, garlic, and salt and cook, stirring, for 8 to 10 minutes, or until lightly caramelized. Add the tomatoes with their juices and wine and continue cooking, stirring frequently, for 10 to 15 minutes, or until reduced by about half.

Add the rice, saffron, and paprika and stir until shiny, about 3 minutes. Add 4 cups [945 ml] of the hot stock, then turn the heat to medium, stir to combine, and season with more salt as needed. Cook, stirring frequently, for 10 minutes.

Add the peas, then stir in most of the seafood, reserving a few pieces of each kind to add later. Turn the heat to medium-high, cover, and cook for 10 minutes, or until the liquid is fully absorbed.

Check the rice for doneness and season with more salt as needed. If the rice is still a bit toothsome, add ½ cup [120 ml] of water or stock and continue cooking. The rice is done when most of it is tender and some of it sticks to the bottom of the pan, resulting in socarrat, the crispy, caramelized rice on the bottom and around the edges of a good paella. The shrimp should be pink in color and no longer opaque, and the fish should flake when poked with a fork.

Add the reserved seafood and squeeze half of the lemon wedges over the paella. Cover and let the newly added seafood steam for 8 to 10 minutes, or until the shrimp are pink and no longer opaque. Chop the reserved green onion stems and parsley leaves and sprinkle over the paella. Place the paella pan in the middle of the table with the remaining lemon wedges on the side and watch your dinner guests devour it.

Pan con Tomate

SERVES 4 TO 6

4 ripe tomatoes, such as Roma, heirloom, or beefsteak

4 to 6 slices crunchy sourdough bread, cut into ½ in [13 mm] thick slices

2 Tbsp high-quality olive oil, plus more for serving

Flaky salt

6 garlic cloves, peeled

1 pint [300 g] cherry tomatoes, halved

Freshly ground black pepper

4 to 6 fresh basil leaves, torn

1 Tbsp chopped fresh oregano

Preheat the oven to 425°F [220°C]. Line a baking sheet with parchment paper.

Cut 2 of the ripe tomatoes in half and grate them on a box grater set in a shallow bowl to catch the purée—the tomatoes won't go through easily, so you will have to push them. You should have about 1 cup (240 ml) of coarse tomato purée. Set the purée aside and discard the tomato skins and seeds

Cut the remaining 2 ripe tomatoes into ¼ in [6 mm] thick slices. Cut the slices in half if they won't fit on the bread.

Brush both sides of the sliced bread with olive oil and sprinkle with salt. Arrange the bread in an even layer on the prepared baking sheet and toast in the oven for about 8 minutes, or until browned and crisp. You can also grill the bread on a grill pan or outdoor grill to add a smoky flavor. Remove the toast from the oven, then roughly rub it all over with the garlic—use almost a whole clove per slice of toast. Spoon the tomato purée evenly over each toast, then arrange the tomato slices and cherry tomatoes on top. Generously sprinkle each toast with salt and pepper and drizzle with olive oil. Top with the basil and oregano and serve immediately.

Flan de Leche

SERVES 8 TO 10

2½ cups [500 g] granulated sugar

2 cups [475 ml] whole milk

1 cup [240 ml] heavy cream

¼ tsp kosher salt

6 large eggs, plus 5 large egg yolks

½ tsp vanilla bean paste or 1 tsp vanilla extract
(I prefer paste here)

In a medium saucepan, combine 1 cup [200 g] of the sugar and 2 Tbsp of water and whisk to dissolve the sugar and make sure none sticks to the bottom of the pan. Put the pan over medium-high heat and bring to a boil, shaking and swirling the pan to combine the sugar and water. Do not stir, as this will cause the mixture to seize. Continue boiling for 10 to 15 minutes, swirling the pan regularly to make sure no sugar sticks to the bottom and to create even caramelization. The caramel is done when it is a deep golden color. Pour the caramel into the bottom of a 9 in [23 cm] round springform pan, about 3 in [8 cm] deep, or divide among ramekins, if you prefer individual servings—this recipe will make about twelve 4 oz [120 ml], eight 6 oz [180 ml], or six 8 oz [240 ml] portions, depending on the ramekin size. Swirl the pan or ramekins to evenly coat the bottoms with caramel. Set aside. The caramel will harden slightly.

Preheat the oven to 325°F [165°C]. Bring a pot or kettle filled with water to a boil.   **cont.**

In a small saucepan over low heat, combine the milk, heavy cream, salt, and the remaining 1½ cups [300 g] of sugar. Warm, stirring, until the sugar is melted. Set aside.

In the bowl of a stand mixer fitted with the whisk attachment, combine the eggs, egg yolks, and vanilla and whip on high speed until smooth. With the mixer on low speed, gradually add the milk mixture in a slow, steady stream. (It's very important to go slowly at first, so the hot milk doesn't cook the eggs.) Mix until smooth, then pour on top of the caramel in the springform pan or divide among the ramekins.

Place a 13 by 18 in [33 by 46 cm] baking dish in the oven, then carefully place the springform pan or ramekins flat in the baking dish. (If you are using ramekins, you can use two 9 by 13 in [23 by 33 cm] baking dishes.) Carefully pour enough of the boiling water into the baking dish to come halfway up the sides of the springform pan or ramekins. Bake for 45 minutes to 1 hour, or until the flan is set but still jiggly in the center. Carefully remove the baking dish from the oven and then carefully lift the pan or ramekins out of the baking dish. Let cool for 30 minutes, then refrigerate, uncovered, until cold and firm, at least 8 hours. The caramel will soften as the flan sits. The flan can be wrapped tightly in plastic wrap and refrigerated for up to 3 days.

When ready to serve, grab a blow-dryer and quickly run it around the edges of the pan or ramekins for just a few seconds. Run a thin, sharp knife around the edges, then center a serving plate, or individual plates if using ramekins, on top of the pan and, holding both the pan and the serving plate, carefully flip everything over together. Lift off the pan or ramekins and let the caramel run all over the top. Serve immediately.

Spanish Red Sangria

SERVES 8 TO 10

4 apples

4 oranges

Two 750 ml bottles dry Garnacha (Grenache) or Shiraz

One 750 ml bottle dry rosado (Spanish rosé) or any dry rosé

1 oz [30 ml] triple sec

One 750 ml bottle Cava

Cut 2 of the apples in half; reserve the rest for serving. Cut 2 of the oranges in half; reserve the rest for serving.

In a large pitcher or container, combine the red wine, rosado, triple sec, and the halved apples. Squeeze the halved oranges into the mixture, then drop the oranges into the pitcher. Stir to combine, then refrigerate for at least 4 hours but preferably overnight.

When ready to serve, cut the remaining apples and oranges into ¼ in [6 mm] wedges. Fill red wine glasses with ice and add 1 wedge of orange and 1 wedge of apple to each. Fill each glass three-quarters of the way with sangria, then top with Cava, stir, and enjoy.

FEARLESS FRENCH DINNER

Like so many chefs and home cooks, I have been profoundly influenced by Julia Child. Before my junior year at Auburn University, I came home for a quick weekend break from summer classes. I felt lost, uninspired, and disconnected from college life. I needed a change. While sitting in a movie theater in Dothan, Alabama, watching Amy Adams burn Julia's boeuf bourguignon in *Julie & Julia*, I dropped out of college on my flip phone. I vowed to chase my dreams like Julia did (in her late forties to boot!), to stop taking life so seriously, and to live fearlessly and unapologetically.

What's wonderful about this Boeuf Bourguignon (and this entire menu) is that it lets us all enjoy the effortless sophistication the French are famous for. Making this dish always gives me a shot of confidence because it's not nearly as hard as it seems in the movies. I swear, y'all, it's just a roast! But you will feel accomplished and proud when you've mastered it. The same goes for the Chocolate Soufflé, which is perfectly French in its rich flavor and simple elegance. I recommend a big, bold French red wine to pair with this meal. If you want a cocktail, try my Big Batch French 75. Here's to conquering your fears and embracing some delicious French cooking!

Boeuf Bourguignon

SERVES 4 TO 6

3 lbs [1.4 kg] cubed chuck beef, at room temperature

Kosher salt

3 bacon slices, chopped

2 cups [180 g] mushrooms, quartered (I like to use cremini or wild)

2 yellow onions, chopped

1 carrot, chopped

2 garlic cloves, minced

1 Tbsp tomato paste

2 Tbsp all-purpose flour

3 cups [710 ml] dry red wine

2 bay leaves

2 fresh thyme sprigs

1 fresh rosemary sprig

2 cups [230 g] pearl onions

4 cups [945 ml] beef stock

4 Tbsp [55 g] unsalted butter

Freshly ground black pepper

1 bunch fresh parsley, leaves chopped, for serving

Using paper towels, pat dry the beef. Season it all over with salt and let stand for at least 30 minutes at room temperature or in the refrigerator for up to 24 hours.

Preheat the oven to 350°F [180°C].

In a large Dutch oven or heavy-bottomed pot with a tight-fitting lid, cook the bacon over medium-low heat for 10 to 12 minutes, or until the fat has rendered and the bacon is slightly browned and crispy. Using a slotted spoon, transfer the bacon to a paper towel–lined plate.   cont.

Place the pot over medium-high heat, add half the beef in a single layer, and sear for 5 minutes on each side, or until well browned all over. Transfer the meat to a plate and repeat to cook the remaining beef. Add the mushrooms to the pot and cook, without stirring, for 2 to 4 minutes, or until browned on one side. Turn the heat to medium-low, then add the chopped yellow onions, carrot, and garlic and cook, stirring occasionally, for 8 to 10 minutes, or until soft. Add the tomato paste, stir, and cook for 1 minute. Stir in the flour and cook for 1 minute, then add the wine, bay leaves, thyme, and rosemary, scraping up any brown bits on the bottom of the pot. Add the pearl onions, beef stock, butter, and 8 to 10 turns of pepper and bring to a boil. Turn the heat off, then return the browned beef and bacon to the pot. Cover the pot, place it in the oven, and cook, turning the meat after about 45 minutes, for 1½ to 2 hours total, or until the meat is tender and the liquid has reduced to a sauce.

As with most braised meat, this dish benefits from resting overnight, so I strongly recommend letting it cool completely and then refrigerating it and reheating before serving to guests. When ready to serve, reheat the boeuf bourguignon in a 350°F [180°C] oven for about 20 minutes, or until hot. Sprinkle with the parsley and serve over mashed potatoes, cauliflower, or rice, or with a side of crusty bread, or alongside the French Potato and Green Bean Salad (page 259).

French Potato and Green Bean Salad

SERVES 4 TO 6

1 lb [455 g] baby yellow potatoes, cut into ¼ in [6 mm] slices

Kosher salt

1 lb [455 g] green beans, trimmed and cut into ½ in [13 mm] pieces

3 Tbsp Dijon mustard

3 Tbsp red or white wine vinegar

2 Tbsp apple cider vinegar

Zest and juice of 1 lemon

3 Tbsp olive oil

1 cup [100 g] chopped green onions, green and white parts

½ cup [20 g] chopped fresh flat-leaf parsley

¼ cup [2 g] chopped fresh dill

3 garlic cloves, minced

8 to 10 turns freshly ground black pepper

In a medium pot, cover the potatoes with water. Add 1 Tbsp of salt and bring to a boil. Continue boiling for about 10 minutes, or until the potatoes are easily pierced with a knife. (Be careful not to overcook the potatoes or they will be mushy.) Drain and rinse with cool water, then leave to drain.

Meanwhile, bring a medium pot of water to a boil. Fill a bowl with ice water. Add the green beans to the boiling water and blanch for 2 to 3 minutes, then immediately plunge them into the ice water to stop the cooking. Drain and set aside.

In a large bowl, whisk together the mustard, red or white wine vinegar, apple cider vinegar, and lemon zest and juice. While whisking, gradually add the olive oil in a thin stream, whisking until fully combined. Add the green onions, parsley, dill, garlic, and pepper, followed by the potatoes and green beans. Toss to coat, then taste for seasoning, adding salt and pepper as needed. Serve warm, chilled, or at room temperature.

Chocolate Soufflés

MAKES TEN 8 IN [20 CM] OR TWELVE 6 IN [15 CM] SOUFFLÉS

12 Tbsp [170 g] unsalted butter, at room temperature
⅓ cup [65 g] granulated sugar, plus more for the ramekins
8¾ oz [250 g] bittersweet chocolate morsels or disks
8 large egg whites
½ cup [60 g] confectioners' sugar, for dusting
Whipped cream, for serving (optional)
Vanilla ice cream, for serving (optional)

Preheat the oven to 400°F [200°C]. Using a pastry brush, generously coat ten 8 in [20 cm] or twelve 6 in [15 cm] ramekins with 6 Tbsp [85 g] of butter. Sprinkle with granulated sugar to generously coat.

In a medium bowl set over a pan of simmering water or in a microwave, melt the chocolate with the remaining 6 Tbsp [85 g] of butter, stirring until combined. Set aside.

In the bowl of a stand mixer fitted with the whisk attachment, whip the egg whites on medium speed, gradually adding the granulated sugar, 1 Tbsp at a time. Continue whipping for at least 5 minutes, or until stiff peaks form. The meringue is ready when the mixture is so stiff that you could hold the bowl over your head without any spilling.

Using a rubber spatula, gently fold the meringue into the chocolate mixture in three parts. Fold until the mixture is smooth and evenly mixed, but do not overmix—the batter should be light and airy. Using an ice cream scoop or piping bag, fill the prepared ramekins a little over halfway with batter. Bake for 8 to 10 minutes, or until the soufflés have risen about ¼ in [6 mm] above the rim. Dust with confectioners' sugar and serve immediately with ice cream or whipped cream, if desired.

Big Batch French 75

SERVES 4 TO 6

12 oz [360 ml] dry gin (I like Bombay or Tanqueray best)

4 oz [120 ml] fresh lemon juice

4 oz [120 ml] simple syrup

One 750 ml bottle Champagne or a dry brut sparkling wine, chilled

Lemon peels or twists, for garnish

Fill a pitcher halfway with ice, then add the gin, lemon juice, and simple syrup and stir until fully chilled. Strain to remove the ice, then serve immediately or cover and refrigerate for up to 1 week.

When ready to serve, add a shot of the gin mixture to 4 to 6 champagne coupes or flutes, then fill with the Champagne or sparkling wine. Garnish with lemon peels or twists and enjoy.

RAMEN SUNDAYS

PART

V

FORMAL AFFAIRS & SLOW FOOD SOCIALS

Ramen is my ultimate comfort food—I love making it, and I love eating it. I've had the privilege of enjoying ramen made by talented Japanese chefs, and moreover, the privilege of learning some of their techniques. Something I love about cooking is that it's an opportunity to be a student forever. In recent years, I would describe my cooking as global but strongly influenced by where I've been and where I'm from. Growing up where I did and with the culinary education I have, the ramen I make is a blend of what I've learned over the years and what comes easily to me—those Southern traditions.

The same goes for the Roasted Apple, Peanut Streusel, and Chili Crunch Ice Cream Sundaes I like to serve with this meal. During my time on *Top Chef*, when I left Dothan, Alabama, known as the peanut capital of the world, and traveled to China, what was I surrounded by? Peanuts! I had no idea that peanuts (and apples) are so popular in China. Y'all, I know the combination in this sundae may sound bizarre, but you have to trust me that it is out of this world. The pairing of peanuts, apples, vanilla ice cream, and chili crunch is an unmatched rollercoaster of flavor and texture and a Pop Rocks–like experience for the palate. Just give it a try, ok? This whole meal is one I love to spend Sunday putting together and savor with my family (and maybe a movie) at the end of the day.

Southern-Style Ramen

SERVES 6 TO 8

Broth

One 3 to 6 lb [1.4 to 2.7 kg] chicken, quartered, or 2 thighs, 2 legs, and 2 breasts (all skin-on and bone-in)

1 smoked ham hock

4 cups [284 g] packed collard greens

2 cups [120 g] dried shiitake or porcini mushrooms

3¼ oz [90 g] cremini or shiitake mushrooms

2 onions, chopped

2 bunches green onions, greens finely chopped and whites reserved for garnish

2 celery stalks, chopped

10 to 12 garlic cloves, chopped

One 2 to 3 in [5 to 7.5 cm] piece fresh ginger, peeled and thinly sliced

4 qt [3.8 L] chicken stock

1 cup [240 ml] soy sauce

¼ cup [56 g] Better Than Bouillon roasted chicken base

2 Tbsp fish sauce

2 Tbsp hoisin sauce or oyster sauce

¼ cup [28 g] Szechuan peppercorns

2 pieces ground star anise, ground

2 pieces ground cardamom, ground

1 cinnamon stick

Toppings

Kosher salt

1 cup [140 g] shelled peanuts

½ cup [120 ml] apple cider vinegar

1 cup [160 g] mustard seeds

One 1 lb [455 g] pork tenderloin

2 Tbsp toasted sesame oil

¼ cup [60 ml] hoisin sauce

1 Tbsp chili crunch, plus more for serving

2 to 3 bok choy heads, leaves separated

½ cup [146 g] pepper jelly

6 bacon slices, chopped

6 to 8 large eggs

12 to 18 oz [340 to 510 g] dried ramen noodles

1 piece nori

4 cups [100 g] pork rinds, crushed

1 cup [227 g] pickled okra, cut into rounds

4 to 6 radishes, thinly sliced

1 bunch fresh cilantro

Reserved whites of green onions

To make the broth: In a large pot over high heat, combine the chicken, ham hock, collard greens, dried mushrooms, fresh mushrooms, onions, finely chopped green onion greens, celery, garlic, ginger, chicken stock, soy sauce, roasted chicken base, fish sauce, hoisin sauce or oyster sauce, peppercorns, star anise, cardamom, and cinnamon. Bring to a boil, then lower the heat to a simmer.   cont.

Continue simmering for at least 1 hour and up to 4 hours, adding water if the broth reduces to less than 10 cups [2.4 L]. You should end up with about 10 to 12 cups [2.4 to 2.8 L] of broth. While the broth is simmering, prepare the toppings.

To blanch the peanuts: In a medium pot, bring 2 cups [475 ml] of water and 2 Tbsp of salt to a boil. Add the peanuts, then lower the heat to a simmer and cook, uncovered, for 30 minutes, or until tender. Drain.

To pickle the mustard seeds: In a small pot, bring 1 cup [240 ml] of water, the apple cider vinegar, and 1 Tbsp of salt to a boil. Add the mustard seeds, then turn the heat to low and simmer, uncovered, for 20 to 30 minutes, or until tender. Drain and set aside.

To cook the pork: Preheat the oven to 450°F [230°C]. Use paper towels to pat dry the pork, then sprinkle all over with salt. In a large skillet or sauté pan over medium-high heat, warm the sesame oil. Add the pork and sear, using tongs to turn the meat, until browned all over, for about 5 minutes total. In a small bowl, stir together the hoisin sauce and chili crunch, then brush on the pork and transfer it to a roasting pan; do not clean the skillet. Roast the pork for 15 minutes. Let rest for 10 to 15 minutes, then cut into thin slices.

To cook the bok choy: Put the skillet used to sear the pork over medium-high heat. Add the bok choy and cook, letting it wilt and get a little color, for 3 to 4 minutes. Transfer to a small bowl, then add the pepper jelly and toss to coat. Do not clean the skillet.

To cook the bacon: Put the skillet used to cook the bok choy over low heat. Add the bacon and cook for 10 to 12 minutes, or until the fat has mostly rendered and the bacon is slightly crispy. Transfer the bacon to a paper towel–lined plate; do not clean the skillet.

To fry the eggs: Put the skillet used to cook the bacon over medium heat. Add the eggs and fry for 3 minutes.

To serve, strain the broth through a fine-mesh sieve into a clean pot; discard the solids. Bring the broth to a boil, then add the ramen noodles and cook for 3 to 5 minutes, or until al dente. Using tongs, remove the noodles and divide evenly among serving bowls. Add the nori to the broth. Pour some broth into each bowl to cover the noodles, then top with all the toppings. Enjoy immediately.

Roasted Apple, Peanut Streusel, and Chili Crunch Ice Cream Sundaes

SERVES 4 TO 6

Peanut Streusel

2 cups [452 g] unsalted butter, at room temperature

2 cups [400 g] granulated sugar

2 tsp kosher salt

3 large egg yolks

1 Tbsp vanilla extract

3 cups [420 g] all-purpose flour

2 cups [280 g] peanuts, blanched (see page 266)

1 tsp ground cinnamon

½ tsp ground nutmeg

½ tsp ground ginger

¼ tsp ground allspice

¼ tsp ground cumin

⅛ tsp fennel seeds

Stewed Apples

¼ cup [50 g] light brown sugar

¼ tsp ground cinnamon

Pinch of ground allspice

Pinch of kosher salt

6 Gala or Pink Lady apples, peeled and cut into ½ to 1 in [13 mm to 2.5 cm] slices

Sundaes

½ gallon [1.9 L] vanilla ice cream

4 to 6 Tbsp [86 to 114 g] chili crunch

To make the peanut streusel: Preheat the oven to 325°F [165°C]. Line a baking sheet with parchment paper.

In the bowl of a stand mixer fitted with the paddle attachment, combine the butter, granulated sugar, and salt. Beat on medium speed, scraping down the sides of the bowl as needed, for about 5 minutes, or until pale yellow and smooth. (Do not beat until fluffy, as you don't want to incorporate air into the dough.) Add the egg yolks and vanilla and mix for 1 minute, or until just combined. Scrape down the bottom and sides of the bowl, then add the flour, peanuts, cinnamon, nutmeg, ginger, allspice, cumin, and fennel. Scrape down the bottom and sides of the bowl again, then mix on low speed for about 1 minute, or until the flour is fully incorporated. The streusel will be in large crumbles.   **cont.**

Spread the crumbles on the prepared baking sheet and bake, rotating the baking sheet every few minutes, for 20 to 30 minutes total, or until light golden and slightly crunchy. (Alternatively, wrap and refrigerate the dough for up to 1 week or freeze for up to 3 months to bake later.) Let cool before using. The baked streusel can be stored in an airtight container in the refrigerator for up to 1 week or the freezer for up to 3 months.

To make the stewed apples: Preheat the oven to 400°F [200°C]. Line a baking sheet with parchment paper.

In a medium bowl, combine the brown sugar, cinnamon, allspice, and salt. Add the apples and toss to coat. Spread the apples in a single layer on the prepared baking sheet and bake for 10 minutes, then toss and bake for another 10 to 20 minutes, or until tender but still firm.

To assemble the sundaes: Spoon 2 scoops of ice cream into each of four to six bowls. Divide the stewed apples, then the peanut streusel among the bowls. Drizzle each sundae with about 1 Tbsp of chili crunch. Enjoy immediately.

HUNTING SEASON

PART

V

FORMAL AFFAIRS & SLOW FOOD SOCIALS

When you live in the rural South, it's not unusual for a friend to show up with a bag from that morning's hunt. Duck and deer sausage are my most favorite gifts to receive, and this hunter's cassoulet has become somewhat of a signature dish of mine. It makes a great Sunday slow food meal in winter. Speaking of the South, it seems only natural to pair this rich stew with a smoky bourbon cocktail. A light, clean, and subtle custard pie provides a great finish to this cozy feast.

Hunting Season Cassoulet

SERVES 4 TO 6

Duck Confit

4 to 5 lbs [1.8 to 2.3 kg] duck quarters (leg and thigh pieces)

6 to 8 garlic cloves

1 shallot, smashed

4 to 6 fresh thyme sprigs

3 to 6 fresh sage leaves

3 fresh rosemary sprigs

4 to 6 whole cloves

4 star anise pods

3 bay leaves, crumbled

3 Tbsp kosher salt

1 tsp juniper berries, crushed with a rolling pin or mortar and pestle

1 tsp peppercorns

7 to 8 cups [1.7 to 1.9 kg] duck fat

Sausage Butter Beans

15 oz [425 g] deer sausage or any other smoky, spicy sausage, chopped

1 onion, chopped

4 cups [640 g] fresh or frozen butter beans

¼ cup [56 g] Better Than Bouillon roasted chicken base

4 cups [945 ml] chicken stock

1 Tbsp fish sauce

1 Tbsp chili crunch

1 Tbsp apple cider vinegar

2 bay leaves

8 to 10 turns freshly ground black pepper

½ cup [75 g] Cornbread Crumble (recipe follows)

To make the duck confit: In a large bowl, combine the duck, garlic, shallot, thyme, sage, rosemary, cloves, star anise, bay leaves, salt, juniper berries, and peppercorns. Toss to coat the duck, then cover and refrigerate for at least 24 hours and up to 2 days.

When ready to braise the duck, preheat the oven to 300°F [150°C]. Remove the duck from the refrigerator, rinse off any excess cure, and pat dry.   cont.

In a large Dutch oven over medium heat, melt the duck fat. Add the duck, skin-side down, and sear until the fat just begins to bubble. Turn off the heat, cover with a lid, and put in the oven to braise for 3 to 6 hours, or until the meat easily pulls away from the bone. (Alternatively, braise the duck overnight in a 200°F [95°C] oven.) Remove from the oven, then carefully remove the duck from the fat and let both cool to room temperature. Discard the fat, or refrigerate in a tightly sealed container for up to 3 months.

Meanwhile, make the sausage butter beans: In a medium Dutch oven or pot over medium-low heat, cook the sausage and onion for about 5 minutes, or until the onion is slightly translucent and the sausage has released its fat. Add the butter beans, roasted chicken base, chicken stock, fish sauce, chili crunch, apple cider vinegar, bay leaves, and pepper and bring to a boil. Lower the heat to a simmer and cook for 15 to 20 minutes, or until the beans are tender but not mushy. Drain the beans.

Once the duck is cool enough to comfortably handle, pull the meat from half of the duck and fold that into the prepared butter beans. Keep warm.

Set a cold cast-iron skillet on the stove and add the remaining duck, skin-side down. Turn the heat to medium-low, cover, and cook the duck, spooning off excess fat as needed, for 10 to 15 minutes to warm it through and crisp the skin. Divide the butter bean mixture among plates or shallow bowls, then top with the crispy-skinned duck and cornbread crumble. Serve right away.

Cornbread Crumble

MAKES ABOUT 4 QUARTS [3.2 KG] OF CRUMBLE

3 cups [420 g] all-purpose flour

2 cups [310 g] fine-ground yellow cornmeal

¼ cup [50 g] granulated sugar

1 Tbsp baking powder

1 tsp baking soda

1 tsp kosher salt

1½ cups [339 g] unsalted butter, cold and cut into small cubes

1 cup [240 ml] buttermilk

1 large egg, whisked

Preheat the oven to 400°F [200°C]. Butter a large cast-iron skillet, casserole dish, or regular muffin tin.

In the bowl of a stand mixer fitted with the paddle attachment or in a food processor fitted with the blade attachment, combine the flour, cornmeal, sugar, baking powder, baking soda, and salt. Add the butter and mix on low speed until the butter is the size of peas. Gradually add half of the buttermilk, then scrape down the sides and bottom of the bowl. Add the rest of the buttermilk and mix just until combined. Remove the paddle attachment or blade and use a rubber spatula to gently fold the batter from the bottom, making sure all the dry ingredients have been incorporated.

Fill the prepared skillet, casserole dish, or muffin tin cups three-quarters of the way with the batter, gently pressing the top to flatten it. Using a pastry brush, brush the top with the whisked egg. Bake until the cornbread is golden and a toothpick comes out clean, 8 to 10 minutes for the muffin tin and 15 to 20 minutes for a large skillet or casserole dish. Let cool on a towel for 10 minutes, or until cool enough to comfortably handle.

Lower the oven temperature to 300°F [150°C]. Crumble the bread onto a baking sheet and bake for 20 to 30 minutes, or until toasted and crunchy. The cornbread crumble can be made ahead and stored in an airtight container in the refrigerator for up to 1 week or in the freezer for up to 1 month.

Egg Custard Pie

SERVES 8 TO 10

1 blind-baked pie shell (recipe follows)
or store-bought if in a pinch (no judgment!)

3 large eggs

½ cup [100 g] granulated sugar

½ tsp kosher salt

Pinch of freshly ground nutmeg

3 cups [710 ml] whole milk

9¼ oz [260 g] fresh berries, sliced figs, or sliced peaches

Whipped cream, for garnish (optional)

Preheat the oven to 400°F [200°C]. Set the blind-baked pie shell on a baking sheet.

In a large bowl, combine the eggs, sugar, salt, and nutmeg and vigorously whisk until completely smooth. While whisking, gradually add the milk in a slow, steady stream and whisk until completely incorporated and smooth. Pour into the pie shell and bake for 20 minutes, then lower the oven temperature to 325°F [165°C] and bake for 30 more minutes, or until the filling is set. Refrigerate the pie until completely cool, at least 2 to 3 hours or overnight.

When ready to serve, cut into slices, top with fruit and whipped cream, if desired, and enjoy.

Classic Pie Dough

MAKES TWO 9 IN [23 CM] PIECRUSTS

1 cup [226 g] unsalted butter, cold and cut into small cubes

3 cups [420 g] all-purpose flour

1 Tbsp granulated sugar

1 tsp kosher salt

In a medium bowl, combine the butter and flour. Freeze for 20 minutes.

Generously flour a work surface.

Put the chilled butter and flour mixture in the bowl of a food processor fitted with the blade attachment. Add the sugar and salt and pulse 8 to 12 times, or until the butter is the size of peas.

While pulsing, pour 6 to 8 Tbsp [90 to 120 ml] of ice-cold water, 1 Tbsp at a time, down the feed tube and pulse until the dough begins to form a ball.

Turn the dough out onto the floured work surface and quickly roll it into a ball, being sure not to handle it too much with your hands. Wrap it tightly in plastic wrap and refrigerate for at least 30 minutes. Alternatively, wrap the dough in a double layer of plastic wrap and freeze for up to 6 months. If using frozen dough, thaw for 1 hour before continuing to the next step.

Unwrap the dough, put it on the well-floured work surface, and cut it in half. Use a rolling pin to flatten and roll out one portion of the dough into a circular disk, rolling from the center to the edge and turning and flouring the dough to make sure it doesn't stick to the surface. Continue rolling out the dough until it is at least 1 in [2.5 cm] wider than the pie dish. Place the rolling pin in the middle of the round of dough, fold the dough in half over the pin, and hold it over the pie dish before unfolding it and fitting it into the dish—it should ease into the pie dish without stretching or pulling. Using a sharp paring knife or kitchen shears, trim any excess dough from the rim of the dish. Crimp the edge or press it with a fork. Freeze for 15 to 20 minutes to chill before blind baking. Repeat this for the other portion of dough or wrap it tightly in plastic wrap and freeze for up to 3 months.

To blind bake the pie crust: Preheat the oven to 400°F [200°C]. Remove the prepared pie shell from the freezer and line it with parchment paper, crumpling the paper first so it easily shapes inside the crust. Fill the parchment-lined shell halfway with dried beans or pie weights. Bake for 15 to 18 minutes, or until the edges are golden. Remove the pie shell from the oven and carefully lift the parchment paper and weights out of the shell. Bake the empty pie shell for 6 to 8 minutes to slightly brown the bottom.

Whiskey Sour

MAKES 2 DRINKS

4 oz [120 ml] bourbon

1 oz [30 ml] simple syrup

2 large egg whites

Juice of 1 lemon

3 or 4 dashes Angostura bitters

In a cocktail shaker, combine the bourbon, simple syrup, egg whites, and lemon juice and vigorously shake for about 1 minute, or until foam forms on the top. Add ice and shake a few more times or until the shaker fogs up from being cold. Strain into rocks, coupe, or martini glasses and finish with a few dashes of bitters.

Acknowledgments

I'd like to dedicate this book to my teams
that have made this dream a reality for me.

MY FAMILY.

You have played every role from therapist to dishwasher
to cook to partners. Y'all are my rock and reason to do
more, love more, and be more present every day.

MY KBC TEAM.

You've rode the waves of this career with me, sailing
forward, catching on to each new idea, making it possible
for me to chase my dreams.

MY PUBLICIST, MANAGER, AND AGENCY TEAM.

You've stepped into my shoes, guiding my visions and
goals for the better. Your counsel, kindness, patience,
and expertise are immeasurable.

MY FRIENDS.

You have inspired this book by sparking the light in my life
daily. Y'all constantly encourage me to celebrate every big
or small thing, happy or hard. What a gift you all are.

Index